VISUAL SCRIPTING

by

JOHN HALAS

In collaboration with

Stan Hayward, Dusan Vukotic, Jiri Brdecka, Samuel Magdoff,
Giselle and Ernest Ansorge, Eino Ruutsalo, Joy Batchelor,
Roger MacDougall, Osamu Tezuka, John Wilson, Gunnar Karlson

Visual Communication Books
Hastings House, Publishers
10 East 40th Street, New York, N.Y. 10016

ISBN 8038-7757-9
Library of Congress Catalog Card No. 76-15849

ACKNOWLEDGEMENTS

I would like to express my sincere thanks to the many of my colleagues round the world who kindly submitted their work for selection and to the Executive Board of ASIFA for choosing me to write and compile this book
John Halas. 1976.

Printed and bound in Great Britain
by A. Wheaton & Co., Exeter

CONTENTS

INTRODUCTION

The subject of visual writing has required clarification for a very long time. What is visual writing? How does it relate to other types of writing? Is there a need for it in animated or other types of film production? Is it a skill, or an art, or combination of both, and how does this activity fit in with the rest of the production process?

This book attempts to answer these intriguing problems with contributions from some outstanding figures in the animated cinema, each of whom sees it from a different viewpoint.

It is to be hoped that all those who are involved, or will be involved in any form of visual communication will be stimulated by the experience of the leading animation artists whose ideas and methods are set down here. The basic objective of their contribution is to provide some concise examples of how a storyboard and preproduction script can be prepared in visual terms. My objective in inviting the contribution of my colleagues is to make film and television producers more visually conscious and to help them to think in terms of pictures from the very first stages of a project. Paying scant regard to this rather simple fact in the preparation of a film, and more especially a television programme has led to more damage than the industry may be prepared to admit.

The intention here is not to establish a formula which lays down whether words or pictures should come to the forefront in a visual project. Such a chicken and egg argument has no place here. But it is reasonable that the problem of relationships between visual content and visual development should be examined, particularly as the majority of films and television programmes start off from verbal material which is not always suitable for visual extension. If nothing other than the habit of thinking in pictures alongside the literary development is achieved this book will achieve its function.

As my colleagues are dealing with their own areas of special interest it might also be valuable to investigate the broader aspect of visual writing and its relationship to other art forms.

Eisenstein, the great Russian director and filmologist in his book *Film Sense* maintained that it is not by concentration of thought on each screen unit's content only that the purpose is reached, but by concentration on the final result of a series of joined screen scene units. By holding firmly to this desired result the validity of each separate unit content will decide its retention or rejection, and the perfect juxtaposition will reveal itself.

Eisenstein's concept of the total effect overriding the segmented elements is an approach on which such masters of animation as Fischinger, Alexeieff, Len Lye and Norman McLaren have based their technique and art from the very beginning. An individual frame is meaningless until that frame is joined to another in continuity. The real content however only emerges when isolated scenes are joined to one another. Screencraft begins to turn into reality when scene is joined to

scene. This brings one to the important matter of the script.

The script is the fundamental organisation of sequential continuity of a play which depends on any progression of time development. If the work involves primary human dialogue as may be the case with a play, naturally the visual flow would be of minor relevance; if, however, the work depends on visual development a specific visual outline in terms of visuals is essential. The verbal description of a visual happening or even visual continuity is a poor substitute for drawings, which in such cases may be far more explicit. During the period from 1940 when film craftsmanship was highly proficient, Eisenstein studied and developed his scene changes, for instance in his film *Ivan the Terrible,* in the form of a storyboard, as did Laurence Olivier in his first film *Henry the Fifth.* Emerging directors, like Alexander McKendrick and a number of Hollywood-based directors and producers, such as Carl Foreman, used the storyboarding approach with scripts and so greatly benefitted preproduction research.

Professionalism depends on creative and technical precision, and a thoroughly prepared script with a visual storyboard certainly assists in achieving this quality. The danger of over-labouring a project is less than the complete lack of preparation for it. This question almost draws a distinction between skill and amateurism. The latter has been the mode among younger film makers who are searching for random effects on the way to establishing a freer cinema. The attraction of unlimited and unrestricted activity may be understandable in the context of an *avant-garde,* hand-held camera shot film involving one or two film makers. Even so, the economics of such an approach is questionable. The degree of wasted material is substantially higher than in a planned assignment.

Such an approach is highly inconvenient, if not impossible, in situations where various other skilful people have to perform under pressure of time and economic circumstances. The director must know what he wants, and a visual script will assist him and can be a quick brief to his crew; he can communicate to them his overall visual concept. As for animated films, the techniques involved in them discount the off-the-cuff approach anyway, since the visuals have to be drawn deliberately and the progression of a film depends on drawing performance as opposed to the guided human performances in a live action film.

The visual storyboard, therefore, can be a well integrated part of the total production process which can define the relationship between the role of visuals, dialogue, character development, music and effects, as well as give definition to the essential time continuity and filmic flow.

These essential elements are emphasised according to the nature of an assignment. In a story film, more attention is given to character development than in an *avant-garde* film where the visual content may play the leading element.

Emotional development in characters is especially relevant in feature films and in animated features it certainly requires special study. Mood building, the relationship between characters, timing of visual or literary points, are just a few matters which must be settled before production can commence, rather than later. Once again, pre-production activities including a visual script would be of great help to achieve the essential objective.

Whether script writing in animated cartoons is a professional activity in its own right depends on the size of the studio and the technical proficiency in a country. In the United States and the USSR the activities in this field warrant the employment of professional visualisers as well as scriptwriters. In Great Britain, in the personalities of Joy Batchelor and Stan Hayward, such activity is based on their specific talent in that particular field, although both direct as well as write. Dusan Vukotic (Yugoslavia), who is a brilliant director, prefers to work on his own scripts, as does Jiri Brdecka (Czechoslovakia) and Ernest Ansorge (Switzerland), who, in fact, works practically on his own. There is a pronounced preference among animators to work from their own scripts, whether they have story sense or not. There is also the desire to establish their own preproduction methods. Through this book it is hoped that the policy of adopting improved methods will be shown as possible in both instances.

The obvious differences must be recognised between the great many possible types of films—ranging from the story films to the diagrammatic type and from experimental to advertising films, each requiring a slightly different approach. Also the technical considerations must be realised, especially with the newly emerging electronic techniques using television monitors, where the visuals may only appear on a television screen as a composite image at the end of the process. Computer animation, again, requires a different preproduction technique to suit the method employed.

Every one of these techniques will, nevertheless, depend on ideas, content, continuity, timing of action, story development, organisation, relationship of elements, co-ordination of performance. The endless variety of possibilities, exciting as they may be, must be fulfilled and turned into reality.

Although story sketches continuity is not unusual in a live action production, it is an exception rather than the rule. By and large the feature film industry is still a literary based operation, at least until the art direction and set and costume design is considered. The first stage to motivate the work in features as a rule, is a book or play which conveys the subject in the form of verbal description. The approach is similar with a television play.

Unfortunately, up to this time, the majority of television writers have been trained as radio writers, which may be good discipline in terms of verbal writing, but has little relation to the visual medium. The established routine for both films and television plays is to commence with a treatment solely in terms of verbal description, then to proceed with a rough script which will eventually be developed to a shooting script. All the way along, not only the dialogue, but the scene changes and scene atmosphere are described verbally as an incidental matter to the performance. There is no doubt that the benefit which the live action film industry and television producers could gain by adopting the extra stage of visual story presentation would be enormous, both in advancing the aesthetic and the technical potentialities of the production as well as lowering its costs.

In the animation industry it is an accepted fact that a well prepared storyboard and properly arranged preproduction plan can save time. Here one can easily swing to the other extreme and make a storyboard so perfectly prepared that it becomes a work of art in itself instead of a means to achieve an end. Many storyboards produced by the Disney organisation for the early feature films of the studio may come into that category. The artwork in these have been so detailed that there was little for the background artist and designer to add. In the case of a sponsored and advertising film a similar position can arise. The storyboard is advanced beyond its proper production function and is used as a selling medium with which to approach a client. In such a case it becomes a presentation tool and the artwork is very likely to need substantial revision before it can become useful for the actual production.

For this reason one must distinguish in the design of a visual script whether it is for an external function which basically becomes a medium of presentation, or an internal function, which is a guide for the production and an actual working plan for a film, on the lines of an architectural blueprint.

It has long been proved that in the majority of productions, especially when other departments are involved, the creation of a working storyboard is the only way that a direction can convey and communicate his experience to others. This fact especially applies to projects involving conversions from other media—for example a play or book—on to the screen.

The screen director's skill, and personal experience are expressed and conveyed in the form of his visual plans within those seconds which each individual shot lasts can unfold in this. Here lies the craft and art of visual scripting.

THE NEW DISCIPLINE

Visual scripting is a comparatively new discipline, in fact as far as the animation industry is concerned it still has to become an established profession. The reasons are clear. Visual communication in the form of cinema or television is a recent development in human expression, an inheritor more from literature than from the visual arts. Literature and plastic arts had a long tradition and centuries of experience. Their forms and techniques are established and played a major role in advancing western civilisation. When cinematography was invented at the beginning of the century it was based predominantly on live photography and for decades too modest in scale to attract writing or visual talents, although later the importance of competent storytelling, as well as inspired photographic skill was gradually recognised and eventually became a profession of its own. Animation remained a technical performance in the hands of comic strip artists, whose sole object was to transpose their characteristic news-strips into moving images. Pictorial considerations did not affect and influence such performances too much. The silent film had a life span of only 25 years before the arrival of sound, and during this period it almost succeeded in establishing itself as a major art form. Such a short period of life did not provide a platform for tradition, but already gave an indication of its potential in drama and comedy through the ingenious work of Griffith, Eisenstein, Chaplin and others. The introduction of sound, while expanding the film's potential further, did not advance it towards becoming an independent visual art form. Words spoken on celluloid were closely related to words spoken on the stage. Story telling became word bound. What was said became more important than pictorial quality. The influence of literature was predominant. And it stayed so until the present day. Today, alongside the very large volume of totally literature-based film, there is also the cult of pure film-craft which does not depend on a borrowed discipline. The work of Fellini, Jancso and Borowczyk is based on organic visual development. Story development is expressed by poetic, powerfully visual imagination. Sight and sound find a natural relationship which is new in the advance of pictorial art. Verbal expression is closely integrated, but used only as one of the elements to achieve the final visual effects. The other elements are continuity, colour, music, sound effects and, of course, the performances of human actors. These are the ingredients of today's visual cinema, an independent art of its own, utilising literature, but not wholly dependent on it.

Creativity in visual scripting therefore requires a somewhat wider skill than the skill of a playwright or novelist. A playwrite primarily conveys his ideas by means of dialogue. The stage tends to be walled in by three sides, and the play is confined to limited geography. If the writer wants to open up the play, he has to do it by artificial means. Today the stage tends to turn to film in the form of back or front projection, to bring in an extra dimension. Novelists tend to describe a situation by words, which of course can carry great power, can stimulate imagination, and can provide a colourful visual description. What they cannot do is to develop a theme purely in visual terms. The strength of film lies in its capacity to open up new prospects in the realm of human expression, to expand reality into and beyond the visible world and subsequently to broaden human experience.

The purest form of visual expression is where the least physical restrictions exist, in animated film. Drawn film can break away completely from physical nature and devote itself to free expression in the purest pictorial terms.

Animation also has the advantage that it is not chained to the optical eye of the photographic camera, which automatically reflects reality. It can penetrate easily to examine the actual processes underlying the physical world, and can visualise the invisible. The difference between external and internal images in the process of time is totally new to the experience of the script writing profession. Here lies its basic difficulty.

The arrival of television and its development as the major force in the communications media has also influenced the field of visual scripting. Not for the better. The need for a large volume of work to fill time accelerated production schedules to such an extent that creativity had to be thrown overboard. Both live action and animation suffered equally under such pressures. Once again, the media turned to professional dialogue writers with no other experience in most cases than writing for the radio. Due to budget limitation the majority of scriptwriters write a television play of one hour's length in one week. Often the same play is rehearsed, produced, and televised within three weeks. The consequence of such speed is such that the work will totally depend on dialogue, which carries the play along with a minimum of mobility. The same position has evolved with television animation programmes, which are usually, in order to fit in with programme schedules, 22 mins. to 26 mins. long, providing (with commercials) half-an-hour's entertainment. The format is usually 26 episodes in a series, and most are based on stageplays, with non-stop dialogue. The animation is confined to simplified lip-sync movement and to limited walk cycles to link sequences. The consequence of this approach is that apart from establishing low standards it blunts the audience's critical appreciation. The public unfortunately are not given enough opportunity to see better material which may lead to the rise of general standards.

A further difficulty arises from the fact that our sense of hearing is not always synchronised with our sense of seeing. Our training gives greater emphasis to our ear than to our eye. The educational system primarily concentrates on printed words with emphasis on literature. The training of the eye is confined to a minority group studying arts and crafts. Yet, we live in a visual age, being influenced by television just as much as by our newspapers and literature. The visual intelligence of the young generation is sharper today than their forefathers' and their capacity of observing pictures at a high speed has increased by looking at television practically from their birth. Looking has become just as normal and valuable an occupation as hearing, but with an increased sense of visual perception. It is a great pity that the majority of material which appears both on cinema screens and on television tends to ignore the obvious shift from literary to visual intelligence, and still lingers on and borrows from media which it has superceded.

It is also regrettable that both television and the film industry still depend on internal information based on words. Scripts are written as if they were stage plays, shots are conveyed with carefully descriptive words. Continuity is explained in terms of chapter headings.

Here is a case to update the process of creativity itself and bring it into line with the visual expression of our times.

THE FORMAT

There are certain basic procedures in any script-writing whether the format is purely verbal or visual. They would depend on their predetermined function and on their subsequent use. For this reason it is essential to realise what medium a script is going to be produced in, and in what technique the production will be made. For instance, a television sequence may be produced in real time shooting which will obviously demand a different form of scripting presentation from a frame-by-frame *avant-garde* production. It is essential therefore to know the following.

a) The medium and technique to be employed.
b) The size of unit a project is carried out by.
c) Length of a project.
d) Financial resources for a production.
e) Time limitation.
f) Layout of the visual script.
g) Equipment employed.

The information obtained through these questions would lead to a format which would lend itself to the most direct form of information for the next step which follows the completion of a script.

Most projects start with either some thumbnail sketches or a type-script page simply stating an idea like this:
Title:

"PROMISE OF THE ATOM"

A First Outline of Contents for a Ten-minute Animated Film.

Part I: The World Before the Atom.

Fire existed in the world before man learnt how to use it. It was a force of destruction which animals feared, but in the Ice Age man learnt to control it and use it to warm his home and his food, and so he survived.

From the water boiled over his fires, man generated steam for hundreds of thousands of years, but it was not until 1764 that young James Watt, who had been watching steam lift the lid of his kettle, made the first steam engine.

Until the coming of steam power, human civilisation had been based on the strength of human muscle, aided by a few domestic animals, levers and pulleys.

From the Egypt of the pyramids to the Spain of the Conquistadors, the world's great empires had been built on slave labour.

The invention of steam power, and the Industrial Revolution which followed it, did more than accelerate the pace of travel and widen the scope of manufacturing—they also accelerated the pace of man's development and widened the scope of his understanding. Between 1800 and 1900 the standards of human life developed further than they had done in the several thousand years preceding.

But this only happened in Europe and North America, where coal, metals and the technical ability to use them existed all together. In terms of industrial power—which had proved itself the basis of human society—the rest of the world was literally an age behind.

All this time electricity had existed in the world, but it was known only as a force of destruction—as lightning.

All this time oil had existed in the world, but it was known only as something that burnt and could be destructive.

By 1900 the technicians of the west had learnt to harness both oil and electricity to generate power, and the world we know to-day is based on this power.

Other projects develop into a more presentable format where both the pictures and the theme of commentary is described verbally. The script on the following page for a combined live/animation science film about future communication is a good example for this format.

A format of a visual script could differ immensely according to its function as described and shown by many of the world's most experienced exponents of this craft in this book, but as a general rule it is an advantage to visualise right from the very start of a project.

Pictures can describe a location better than words and can create an atmosphere as well.

If the visual writer is the director it is an advantage to provide him with as much information as possible. The description of characters also works better in pictures than words.

Title:

"PROSPECT A.D. 2000"

Program title: First part

"Machines with Human Minds"

Music, created by Computer, takes over.

Sequence 1. Chess: Man Challenges Machine

Pictorial presentation:	*Theme of commentary:*
Expositor discovered playing chess with a computer, starting in long shot to establish the size of the computer and ending in close shot of expositor concentrating. He makes a move, slowly and deliberately. The machine responds immediately.	*During concentration on expositor, "inman" music takes over.* *Closing phrase of computer music*
As camera pulls slowly back to show player and machine . . . Interior of section of the computer showing some form of working movement. Back to scene, expositor, chess-board, background of computer.	*Expositor spoken thoughts:* *This game has been going on for some time. I'm playing chess with an electronic computer, matching my human brain with its wholly mechanical brain. We know how this computer's brain works . . . because we invented it, and prepared it in advance to respond to every logical move in the game of chess . . . I am already getting tired, but this computer can go on playing until it either breaks down or wears out . . .*
Dissolve to animation; expositor still speaking. Silhouette of expositor's head becomes his brain. A comic figure (the brain gremlin) mimes to expositor's words. "Thinks" position; yawns; twiddles thumbs; swipes fly; resumes "thinks" position again. It sleeps.	*We have still a great deal to find out about how the human brain works. We know its inventive capacities. And we know our human limitations. We get bored. We get distracted. We need sleep.*
close-up expositor's forehead. Pull back as we see he makes a decision. He makes a move against the rules, and looks up to watch what the machine will do.	*Expositor: My brain tells me I can't win; the computer has all the answers. But I wonder what would happen if I were to disobey the set rules (or cheat).*
Computer's cancelling reaction; message thrown up.	*Protecting burst of computer music.*
Close-up of message.	*Expositor: You see, the mechanical brain of the computer can't cope with an emergency in the same way as a human brain would do. It can only do what we have prepared it to do. (He reads the message aloud.)*

The co-ordination of story developmeut with time development in terms of seconds should also be essential.

Finally, it must be remembered that a visual script is not an end product of its own unless it becomes a means of presentation to a sponsor or a client. A teleplay may contain a lovely description of the location in a poetic language which may be wasted in the translation to full production. On the other hand a student made film with no script or storyboard could swing to the other extreme and will inevitably hold up its making half-way through the production. Since film making is an expensive pastime it is far more economical to assure the smooth operation of many of its stages at the start than during its completion. If it is necessary, a storyboard should be reworked time and time again until it is functional and acceptable for production.

John Halas
London 1976

1. VISUAL GRAMMAR: SERGEI EISENSTEIN

John Halas (G.B.)

"DIRECTIONS BECOME DRAWINGS—THE VOICES OF VARIOUS CHARACTERS ARE DRAWN AS SERIES OF FACIAL EXPRESSIONS WHOLE SCENES FIRST TAKE SHAPE AS BATCHES OF DRAWINGS BEFORE THEY TAKE ON THE CLOTHING OF WORDS".

Eisenstein stated the above notes in "Film Form" while he was directing *Ivan The Terrible* in 1941. He was not the first director in need of visualising his thoughts and clarifying his ideas in terms of drawing. Carl Mayer, the Austrian born writer, did it in 1919 for the film *The Cabinet of Dr. Caligari.*

The media of film and now television create the necessity of visualisation. The question is, at what stage should it take place? There are directors who feel the necessity right at the beginning, at the conception of an idea. Others prefer a stage later, after a full verbal treatment of the film project. There are those who wait to visualise until the shooting starts, and many who leave the matter entirely to their camera man, or in the case of the animated film to the designer—the extreme case is when directors do not bother at all and leave it to happen entirely by chance. This method however could not be adopted in animation, since the work itself consists of a series of drawings. It is not a coincidence that most of the outstanding directors of cinema, first Eisenstein, then Fellini, were trained to be artists first. Others like Cocteau, Renoir and Borowczyk in fact were artists and designers first before turning to film-making. They had the advantage of a visual training which proved most advantageous in dealing with the complex nature of film. In the meantime they successfully broke away from the limitations of the static image, and expanded it in the limitless time potential of cinema, adding a new dimension to it.

Eisenstein was a true pioneer, whose position in the history of cinema became unique, not only for his theoretical teaching of a new technique but also because of the films he made. He is still the only Russian film maker who could be compared with Gogol, Dostoyevsky, Tolstoy and Gorki by using true capabilities of the modern medium of cinematography to convey deep human emotions on a vast scale and in great depth. His teaching was not confined to Russian alone. It helped to better understanding of the nature of film and raised its standards. His belief that preproduction work in terms of visual sketches and storyboards should be developed side-by-side with written scripts helped to establish what is known today as "Visual Grammar". By understanding and practising the new language, he was able to bridge the two disciplines, words and images or sound and sight into something new.

In order to achieve results, he introduced many novel concepts into his production. The Big Close-Up for instance was one of them. Although D. W. Griffith actually used this method in his *The Birth of a Nation* it was Eisenstein who made the best use of it. Superimposition of images or montage was another device adopted. The conception of rhythmical editing was especially evident in his film *The Battleship Potemkin* and was also new at the time. The speed of each shot had a physical significance as well as a meaning behind it. The continuity had a rhythm of its own providing a shock tactic. Each step had a specific function.

The final effect was planned with a clear objective in mind—to provide a deep emotional audience involvement. The synthesis of story, technique and new forms was a highly complex intellectual and technical feat which had to be worked out beforehand. But Eisenstein was a superb film architect and his blueprint for a film ensured the structural solidity of his productions. Creativity was given a free hand during the shooting of a scene and in the editing stage.

Eisenstein's insistence on preproduction planning was to solve many of the complex problems during the actual production. The problem of composition, camera angles (he had a masterly sense for composition), the visualisation of literary ideas and verbal meanings, the continuity of scene development, the structural arrangement of sequences, and the timing of the action. All of these can add immensely to the time and cost of any film project if not solved at the right time and in proper relation with each other before the physical filming commences. With visual scripting the problems can be pinpointed at the earliest stage.

There are two basic methods of making films. One is the Eisenstein formula of creative preproduction planning. The other is the free employment of camera (mainly handheld) in search of random effects. The first is more suited to the fluid film medium whereby the participants are obliged to manipulate the extent of time development that the film is subjected to. Film has a beginning and an end. Its development progresses over seconds, minutes, hours—thousands and thousands of film images. The random effects have to be preplanned in order to achieve the maximum result. This is in contrast to the individual artist, whose objective is not so complex. Picasso once said "I do not seek—I find". He may have expressed accurately the method of an artist working on a single picture. Exploration into unknown regions is more possible, if the involvement is by the individual instead of a large unit. Paul Klee goes even further in his search for random effects. He said "The artist knows a great deal, but he knows it only after the event". An individual artist therefore can use his own time to search, to grope. His failure will not hurt anyone. A film director cannot indulge in such luxury, not only on account of artistic and technical procedures, but also on account of simple economics. When during the early 1960's the handheld film technique became popular, it proved to be the most expensive way of making a film. This is especially true in the case of films depending on a developing theme with a

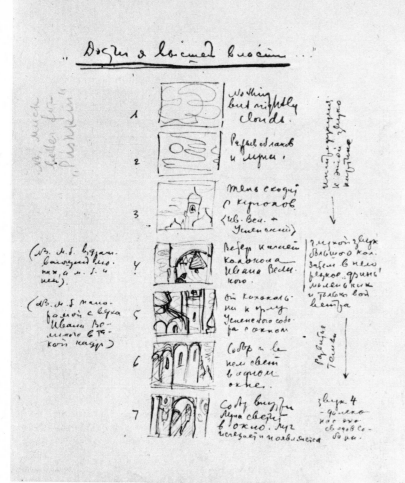

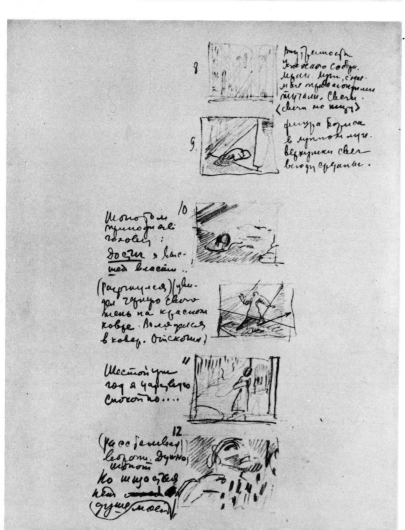

I ATTAINED THE HIGHEST POWER

Introduction to this sound picture.

much better for "Pushkin"

1. Nothing but nightly clouds.

2. A shot (lit.cut) of the clouds and the moon.

(May be in the distance a quivering (trembling) monk but may be not.)

3. The shadow moves from the cupolas (of Ivan Veliky) and Uspensky cathedrals)

Muffled noise of the great bell. Then there is a sharp "ding" of the little bells and on the howl of the wind.

4. The wind rings the bell of Ivan Veliky.

(May be a panorama from above of Ivan Veliky in such a frame)

5. From the bell tower to the eagle of the Uspensky Cathedral together with the window

Development of the theme.

6. The cathedral and a light in one of its windows.

7. The interior of the cathedral. The moon shines through a window. A ray disappears and reappears.

Sound 4.

The echo of the vaults (arches) of the cathedral was carried a long way.

8. Interior of the Uspensky Cathedral. The rays of the moon are being eaten up by the penetrating storm clouds. Candles. (The candles are along the bottom)

9. The figure of Boris in a ray of the moon. The tops of the candles are everywhere cut off.

10. In a whisper after he raised his head : I have attained the highest power. . . . (He straightened up) (he saw his own black shadow on the red carpet. He stared hard at the carpet. Jumped back).

11. I have now been reigning peacefully for six years.

12. (Unbuttoning his collar. It's stuffy) But there is no happiness in my soul.

Sergei Eisenstein
Storyboard for *Boris Godunov*

A cut. *Is it not so—*
We since our youth have lost our hearts, have
thirsted
For the joys of love, but we have only satisfied
The angry hunger by its momentary possession,
Now having grown cold, we are bored and
languishing.

But all this bit up to "in vain" is retained without words
to the corresponding length.
N.B.2. Without remembering the existence of these lines
I earlier had thought between "my" and "in vain" to make
the length equal to the length of the path through the
empty cathedral. In such a passage - the melody of these
lines, but I correctly remove the words, which fall from
the directness of the playful treatment of this scene
(if you like - cinema-primitiveness is unavoidable in
cinematography.

13.

14. *he runs for a long time through such a maze.*
Each pillar surrounded by candles.

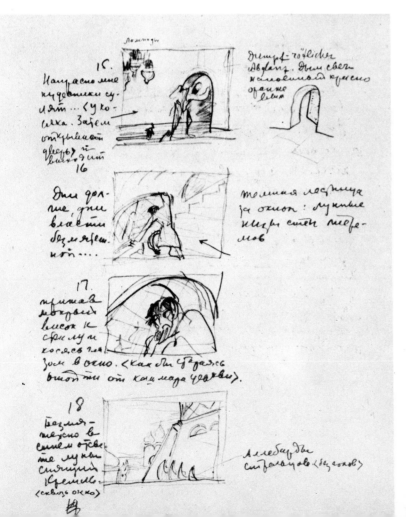

icon-lamps

15. *In vain do the sooth-*   *Dumpf-rötlicher Abglanz*
sayers promise me ...   *(Dull red reflection.) The*
(Stands at an angle. Then   *smoke of the candles fills*
he opens the door and   *[it] with an orangey-red*
goes out.)   *light.*

16. *Long life and days of*   *A dark staircase beyond the*
tranquil power ...   *windows : the moon's rays*
    along the bottom of the
    walls of the terem.

17. *Having pressed his damp*
cheek to the pane and
looking sideways out of
the window (as if
trying to get away from
the nightmare of the
church)

18. *The sleeping Kremlin is*   *The halberds of the streltsy*
serene in the blue   *(their heads cannot be*
reflection of the moon   *seen)*
(through a window)

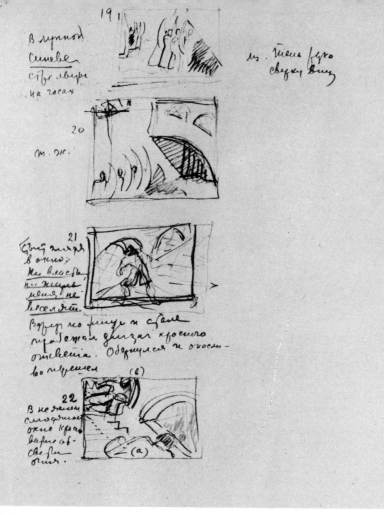

19. In the dark blue light of the moon the streltsy are on guard.

Shadow

20. DITTO.

21. (Stands looking out of the window)

Neither power nor life make me happy

Suddenly along the face and the wall ran the zigzag of a red reflection. He turned round and cautiously crossed over.

(b)

22. In the unclear looking window the ruddy reflection of a fire.

(a)

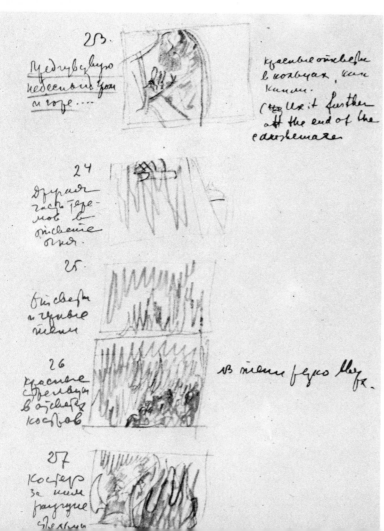

23. I have a foreboding of heavenly rage and grief.

Red reflections in rings, like stones.

(Use it further at the end of the nightmare)

24. Another part of the terems in the reflection of the fire.

25. Reflections and black shadows.

26. The red streltsy in the reflections of the fires.

rarely in view

27. The fire and behind it the streltsy.

Terem—the guard house/ tower

streltsy—At this time—a company of soldiers

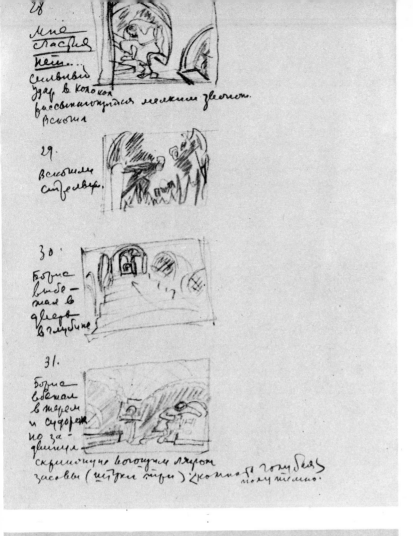

28. There is no happiness
for me . . .

*A strong blow on the bell
dispersing in small sound.
Jumped up.*

29. *The archers jumped up.*

30. *Boris ran out to the
door in the distance.*

31. *Boris ran into the
terem convulsed but
the guards had shut it
with a scraping,
howling clang. (three
pieces). (A blue room
half dark)*

32. *Closing the door with
all my might I thought
my people contented,
calm in glory.*

   *But I've put aside the
   empty care:
   The living power for
   the mob is hateful.
   They know only how
   to love the dead—(he
   went from the frame on
   the left)*

33. *(going up, sitting down)
Stupid we are*

——
——
——

   *(gets up) the people
   moaned perishing in
   torment (examining the
   doors of the orange
   room)*

34. *I opened up the
granaries for them
(forte)*

35. *I gold*

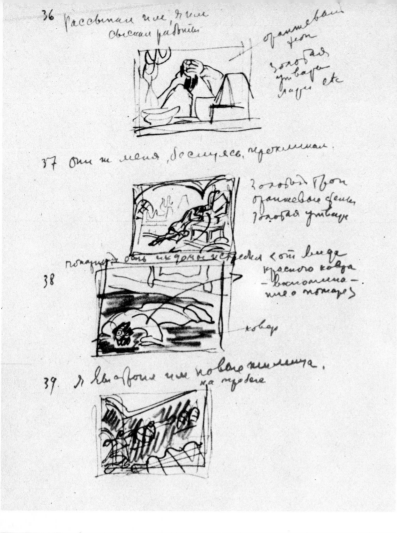

36. scattered to them, I   Orange background,
    found work for them.   golden utensils, coffers etc.

37. They cursed me, raging   Golden throne,
                                  Orange walls,
                                  Golden utensils.

38. The fiery fire has destroyed their homes (the sight of
    the red carpet—reminded—me of the fire).

39. I built new living   —carpet.
    quarters for them.
    on the run

40. (crescendo)   red wall
    But, ME, they blamed
    for the fire
    (broken down):
    This is the rabble's
    judgement: seek, then,
    it's love

41. very quietly and as if
    calmed down (thought
    of his daughter)
    In my own family I
    thought to find joy.

42. I daughter ....   Violet room (the bedroom)
    ....   almost dark yellow rays
    ....   chapel
                    widow

    (gets up)

    Me, me
    unhappy father
    (hurls himself into
    prayer)

43. (breathing over the   Through the ring of the
    lectern)   icon lamps blinded by the
    Whoever it is who dies,   golden frames of the icons
    I am the secret killer
    of everybody
    (foaming)

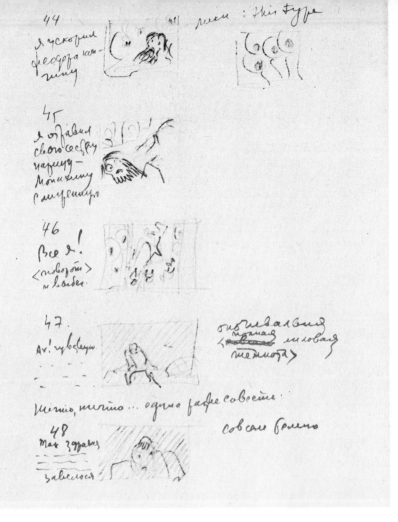

44. I hastened Feodor's   images : this type
    death

45. I poisoned my sister
    the tsaritsa—a humble
    nun

46. I did it all!
    (turn)
    and ran away

47. Ay! I feel   the bedroom, full of
    ....   violet darkness
    ....
    nothing, nothing . . .
    only except conscience

48. So, clear ....   quite dark
    ....
    ....
    appeared

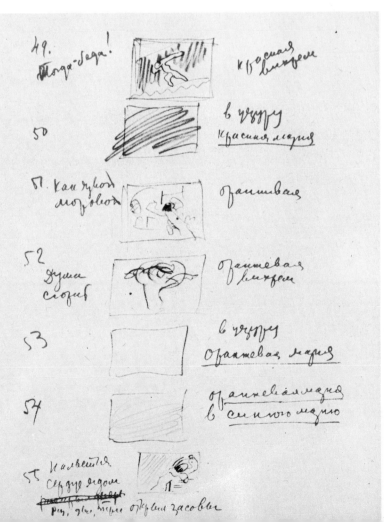

49. Then - misfortune!   red in a whirl

50.   in
                                 red oiliness

51. like a plague   orange

52. the soul will burn up   orange in a whirl

53.   orange oiliness

54.   orange oiliness into
                                dark blue oiliness

55. the heart will be
    filled right up with
    poison
    one, two, there he
    opened the bolts

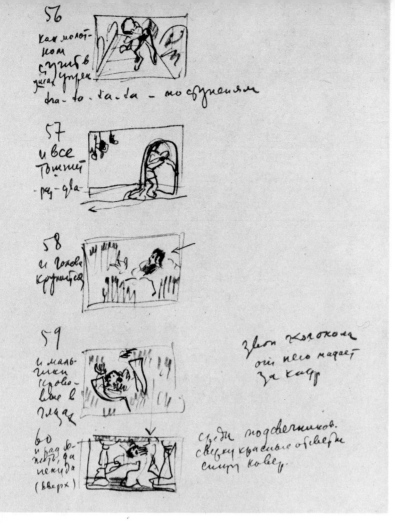

56. *Like a hammer*
the reproach beats
in the ears
tra-ta-ta-ta-down the
steps

57. *and all the time there*
is a sick feeling
one-two

58. *and the head spins*

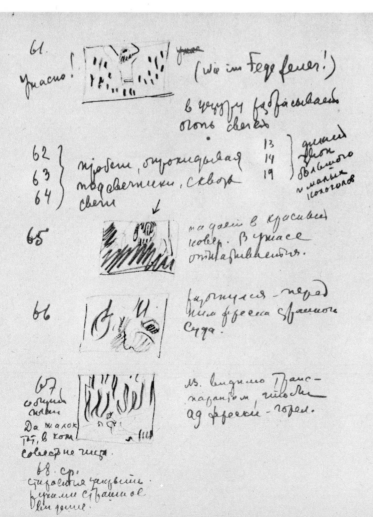

61. *It is terrible!*   (as in Fegefeuer!)
in - he scatters the
fire of the candles.

62.	overturning the	13.	long sound of
63.	candle holders,	14.	big and little
64.	through the light	19.	bells

65. *falls onto the red carpet. In terror thrusts himself*
away

66. *straightens up—in front of him fresco of the dreaded*
court

67. *Yes, pitiable is he whose*   *Evidently with a trans-*
conscience is not clear   *parency so that the hell*
fresco - burned

68. *wipes away with his*
hands the terrible
vision

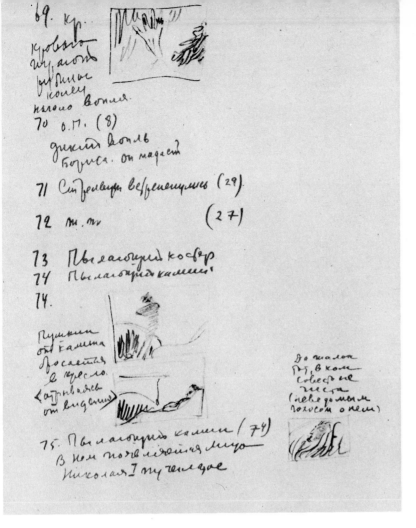

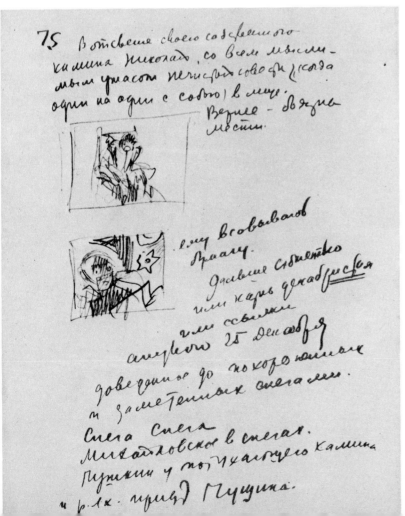

69. The red rubies play
bloodily end and
beginning of a howl

70. O.P. (8)
A wild howl from Boris.
He falls.

71. The streltzy rouse
themselves   29)

72. The streltzy rouse
themselves   27)

73. A burning fire

74. Burning stove. Pushkin   Yes, pitiable is he whose
hurls himself from the   conscience is not clear
stove into a chair   (in an unknown voice
(tearing himself away   about him)
from the vision)

75. Burning stove.
In it there appears the
face of Nicholas I with
goggle eyes.

75. In the reflection of his own (stove) Nicholai with all
the thoughtful terror of an unclean conscience (when
one is alone with oneself) in the face

It is truer - he is afraid of
revenge they thrust a
paper at him

further subject
either the execution of the
Decembrists or the exile.
Anyhow 25th December led
up to the burials and
coverings up by the snows.

Snows, snows
Mikhailovsky in snows.
Pushkin by the dying
stove and arrival of
Pushchin.

direct storyline, which just does not lend itself to improvisation. Eisenstein's attention to the fundamental problems of visual flow, continuity in terms of pictorial development, an analysis of how a shot can anticipate the next one in order to build an effect, did not make him a dictator. Preprojected camera angles and scene composition is natural in animation through the work of a layout artist. In live action it helps to achieve better results and saves a lot of money. Eisenstein still left ample manoeuvrability to his cameraman and crew and was most open-minded with his editor. He was an inspired conductor who gave the right cue to his orchestra.

We have been fortunate to discover and publish here Eisenstein's storyboard for his film project *Boris Godounov* which was previously dramatised on the stage by Pushkin with music specially composed by Mussorgsky. Unfortunately the film itself never got off the ground, but Eisenstein's story-

board appears to be an excellent example of inspired preproduction visual writing.

Eisenstein's artistic creation starts with his early drawings and notes. Ideas are born in close relationship to both at this stage. There is already a clear evidence of his awareness of all the technical problems which may arise in the final production. The mood is already defined. The continuity from one sequence to another is established. The acting style is implied. The choreography of actor's movement is laid out. At this embryonic stage of planning there is hardly any difference between a project for a live or animated film. Obviously subsequent stages in actual production would depart into different lines of action. Eisenstein spoke many languages fluently including English. It is interesting to note that in his storyboard he mixes Russian with English as well as German. Thanks are due to Mr. Bert Pockney of the University of Surrey who translated the text into English.

2. SCRIPTWRITING FOR ANIMATION: THE BASIC APPROACH

Stan Hayward (G.B.)

Stan Hayward has specialised in writing for many types of animated film from TV sports to scientific mathematic films.

His contribution is a penetrating analysis in the definition of the scale that a scriptwriter must undertake in approaching film subjects.

It is hoped that his outline will serve as a useful guide for the many types of film he refers to, as well as some hints on the pitfalls which should be avoided.

Generally speaking, your job as an animation scriptwriter will start with the idea for the film and end with the accepted storyboard.

You will be concerned with *content*: what the film has to say, and *presentation*: how the film is going to say it.

The content will come from the sponsor, his advisers and your own researches. The presentation and styling will come from the director, the designer and your own suggestions.

Everything that goes into the storyboard must satisfy both sponsor and director. It is your job to understand the needs and problems of both.

Briefly, here is how you go about that job:

1 Define the statement of the film in one sentence.
2 Collect as many facts as possible.
3 Order your facts in degrees of importance.
4 Pick out the three or four key points.
5 Illustrate these as simply as possible.
6 Add lesser facts until the key points are easily understood.
7 Collect constructive comments from those involved in the film.
8 Start again.

Aim at solving the content problem first. From this the styling and presentation often become obvious.

An analysis of the film *What is a Computer?* will show how a specification for a film is arrived at.

DEFINING THE STATEMENT

The following questions were asked:
1 What does the film have to say?....(Content)
2 Who does it have to say it to?......(Market)
3 What is it related to?........(Teaching context)
4 How and where will it be shown?....(Format)
5 How long will it be?........(Distribution slot)
6 What is the budget?..........(Full or limited animation)

CONTENT

Several suggestions were put forward. These were shortlisted to:

1 A history of computers: Counting from primitive man up until today. This would have a strong mathematical bias which would limit it to schools.
2 Applications of computers: their use in management decision making, science and automation.
  This would be competing with the many documentary programmes on T.V., and is a subject that dates very quickly.
3 The workings of a computer: How words and numbers are converted into signals, processed, stored, and retrieved.
  This is an area that needs most explaining to most people, it is also dealing with abstract ideas that can be handled well by animation.

The workings of a computer became the statement of the film. This to some extent helps to define the audience.

MARKET

Who would be interested in seeing such a film?

1 The general public.
2 Schools.
3 Industry.

These three major markets are to some extent incompatible.

A film for the general public would have to be mainly entertaining with the education aspect as secondary.

A film for industry would have to be too specialised, and for a very small market.

A film for schools seemed the best market for such a film, but schools fall into three main groups: 8–11 year olds, 12–16 year olds, and university level.

The 12–16 year group was chosen as virtually everyone in this group has to learn something about computers in today's syllabus.

Having decided that this area was our market, the next step was to examine what is being taught at this level by other means.

This brings us to the:

TEACHING CONTEXT

1 Books.
2 Visual aids—films, T.V.
3 Actual use of computers in school.

With the aid of a teaching consultant, we were able to define what was being taught, how it was being taught, and how it was being accepted by the students.

This showed that there were several gaps in the syllabus that a film could usefully fill.

The next question to be answered now that we had the basic information was how to present it. Teaching films can be terribly dull when they are used as an extension of classroom techniques of book or blackboard.

Animated teaching films fall into four main groups:

PRESENTATION

1 Straight diagram with off-screen commentary (or silent).
2 Live-action with animated inserts. Off-screen commentary for animation with, probably, live-action commentator on-screen.
3 Mixed styling that uses live-action, models, still photos, still drawings, and animation. Commentary off-screen.
4 All animation using both characters and diagrams. Commentary varying from scene to scene.

Considering the complexity of the subject, a straight diagram approach was suggested, but styled with comic-book lettering and colouring to make it appeal to children of a lower age group than our original market of 12–16 years. This was done because as teaching methods improve, subjects get taught earlier and earlier. By appealing to a wide group of children, we gave the film a longer life.

As an afterthought, some gags were added to give it a greater entertainment value, and a sequence on management to make it have some limited appeal to industry. In this way at a little extra cost the market could be considerably extended without detracting from our original specification.

Having decided that the market was schools, but with possible wider applications, the next thing to decide on was:

FORMAT

1 Large screen 35 mm.
2 Small screen 16 mm./8 mm.
3 TV screen/8 mm. projector.

In this case, 16 mm. was considered the best format, but bearing in mind that more and more films will be shown on the TV screen, or transferred to cassettes eventually, the design was based on the TV field size. This meant that the backgrounds were virtually eliminated.

We had now reached a specification for the films:

1 The workings of a computer.
2 Aimed at 12–16 year olds but styled for general appeal.
3 Based upon existing school syllabus but not tied to it.
4 Mainly diagram but characters added for humour. Treated as a comic book presentation.
5 Designed for small screen.
6 Full animation.
7 Length, 10–15 min. (This was left open until the storyboard had been fully drawn up and timed).

Of course there are a number of types of computer, and they work in different ways. On advice, we chose the electronic digital computer.

The film had now arrived at a full outline. It was about how an electronic digital computer works. The key facts were:

1 Before symbols can be fed into a computer they must be translated into the binary code.
2 The binary code has only two digits 1 and 0.
3 1 and 0 can be converted into on/off signals.
4 These signals can operate lamps, switches, magnets.
5 These signals can be processed and stored.
6 These signals can be retrieved and translated back into symbols.

This is what the film was about.
The next step was to get down the simplified drawings of these facts.

Simply showing how the computer worked would make a very dull film. Every machine has a philosophy behind it. Someone thought that it would be a benefit to mankind, and in some way fulfilled a need. This philosophy needs to be implied in the way the machine is used.

Starting with the film's philosophy, plus the facts, we arrived at the film's *key points*. There are three key points in any film. If your audience comes away remembering them then your film is a succes.

In the computer film the key points were:

1 What are we dealing with (why do computers exist)? . . . . The information explosion.
2 How is it (*information*) dealt with? . . . . Computerised.
3 To what end? . . . . Calculating, Communicating, Controlling.

It often takes a considerable amount of work to arrive at the key points, but once they are down the rest of the writing is easy. It is a good idea to start out guessing at your key points, and modify your guesses as your facts take on an order.

You have to bear in mind that your purpose is not just to get the facts on to film, but to present some ideas in a clearly defined, entertaining, and memorable way. It just happens that you are using film to do it.

Making a film entertaining and memorable is often difficult enough. At this point we considered poetic licence—how much freedom we had within the film.

In this case, as much of the working was technical and needed to be reflected upon, we felt that anything giving more impact to the words on the screen, would be of value. We gave the letters a personality and made them bounce, slide, roll, jump, flash, change colour etc. This took the film into the area of pure animation, and made it look quite different from a text-book or blackboard approach.

The storyboard was now drawn up. The facts were checked, the styling agreed upon, and key designs drawn, but there was still writing to do. The script had to be ready and storyboard notes are seldom good for reading. The script has to sound right for whoever is reading it—natural and convincing as if the commentator was telling you personally about something that he is interested in. It should not sound like someone standing in a soundproof box, alone, reading from a script that he has never seen before. In the above film the actor had the storyboard two weeks before the recording, and was allowed to make minor alterations in working to suit his own style.

Titles and credits are not always included in the storyboard, and in the film often look as though they were put in as an afterthought. In the computer film, the titles were made by computer. This gave them a styling that anticipated the subject.

The end credits came on via the devices that had been used in the film, so that in a way, they summed up what had been said. It also left the viewers with the film's message in their minds rather than a string of meaningless names. The film should be working for you from the moment it starts until the last frame.

When the storyboard is finished you should go through it with the designer and director to make sure that they understand why you have done what you have done. Although this seems an obvious step, it is not always done thoroughly. I have known consultants to pass over incorrect drawings assuming they would be correct in the finished film—and they weren't! I have also seen art directors design from storyboards without considering transitions implied in the storyboard notes.

A slight oversight can cause an expensive reshoot.

WHERE DOES THE WRITING END?

If you expect the film to come out like the storyboard then it is your job to make sure everyone working on the film understands it.

There is no point in assuming that the editors think the same noises as you when you put a sound effect in. Nor do animators have time to check technical details of drawings roughed out on the storyboard.

The producer assumes you have got your facts right, and the director assumes that you can supply him with source material if he needs it.

You should see that everyone making decisions on the film gets a copy of the storyboard: the client, the producer, the director, the designer, the animator, the editor, the commentator. They should be able to make their comments before the film goes into production.

The scriptwriter's job has really finished at this point, but it is very likely that phrases in the commentary can be interpreted in several ways. It is not always obvious from the storyboard, and it is unlikely that the scriptwriter will be at the recording to check. The easiest way to overcome this prob-

lem is to record it yourself on a tape recorder. However badly you do it, it will be a guide to the director on interpretation.

The same thing applies to the animation. The right gestures and movements can reinforce a scene, the wrong ones can kill it, it is rarely self evident from the storyboard exactly what the gestures are. You should act out the gestures with the animator and let him amend the storyboard while you are there.

The film *What is a Computer?* did not have a well-defined market to begin with; this meant that compromises in length, styling, and market had to be accepted. This does not apply to most animated films like advertising commercials, film titles, entertainment shorts and those that fit an accepted format. But, in spite of the few limitations, not everyone uses the subject and film elements efficiently.

To be efficient means examining every dot, line and colour that goes on the screen and asking if it is working for you.

Here is how to do it.

GENERAL APPROACH TO ANIMATION SCRIPTWRITING

Every film should both entertain and inform. There is no such thing as a dull subject; there are only dull film makers.

A well made film uses space and time efficiently. *Special elements* in order of importance are:
Movement
Colour
Shape (silhouette)
Form (3-dimension)
Line (edges)
Texture

This is the order in which the eye sees them.
Time elements in order of impact are:
Sound effects
Music
Voice

The ear accepts sound effects immediately, but the voice has to be reflected upon.

Dynamics are:
Speeding up
Slowing down
Enlarging
Diminishing
Reversing

Design control:
Simplifying
Generalising
Abstracting
Highlighting

The above elements are changing from frame to frame, but they should only change when they are saying something.

Harold Whitaker
Stan Hayward
John Halas
First storyboard for a science film entitled *Topology* part of a series of films about modern mathematics (pages 24-26).

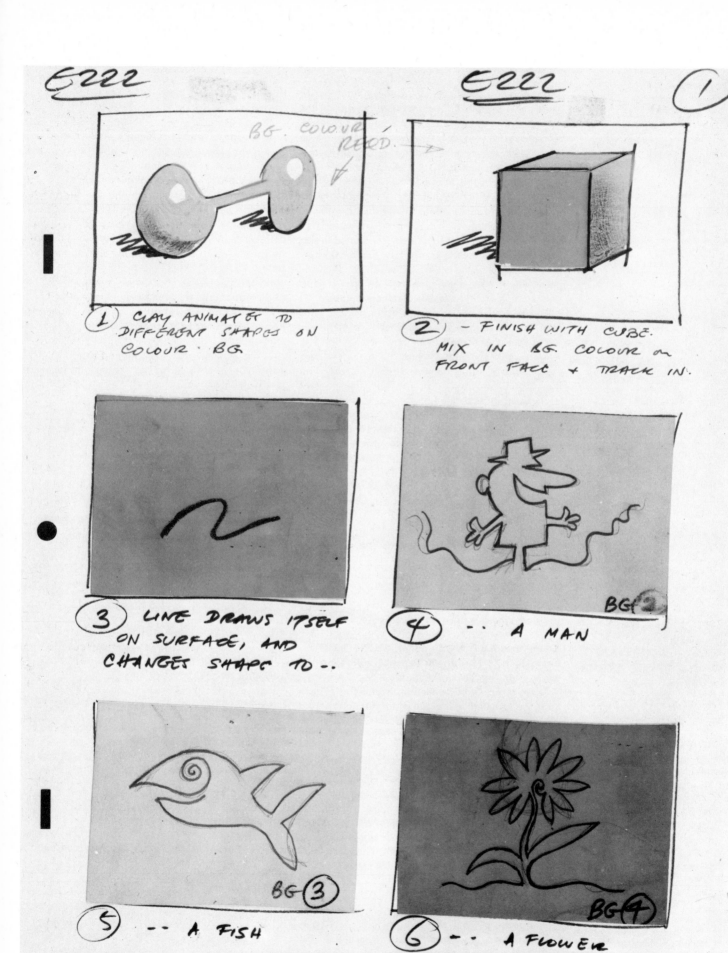

BG. COLOUR
REFD.

① CLAY ANIMATES TO
DIFFERENT SHAPES ON
COLOUR BG

② — FINISH WITH CUBE.
MIX IN BG. COLOUR on
FRONT FACE + TRACK IN.

③ LINE DRAWS ITSELF
ON SURFACE, AND
CHANGES SHAPE TO—

④ — A MAN

BG②

⑤ — A FISH

BG③

⑥ — A FLOWER

BG④

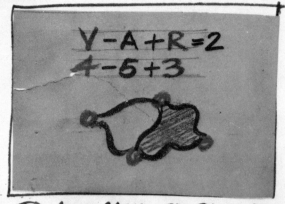

$$V - A + R = 2$$
$$4 - 5 + 3$$

⑦ MIX BACK TO THIS BG.
AS LINE ANIMATES TO
NETWORK

⑧ MAN VISITS BARS ETC
— BG. COLOUR AS ⑦

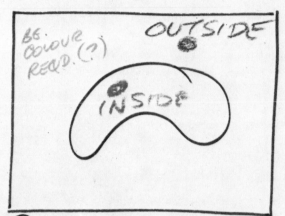

BG.
COLOUR
REQD. (?)

OUTSIDE

INSIDE

⑨ CHANGE OF BG.
COLOUR FOR ⑨,⑩+⑪
(?)

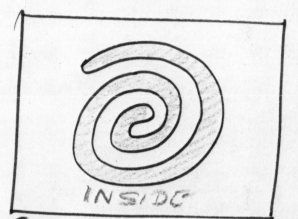

INSIDE

⑩ F/I TINT + LETTERING.

OUTSIDE

⑪ F/I TINT + LETTERING.

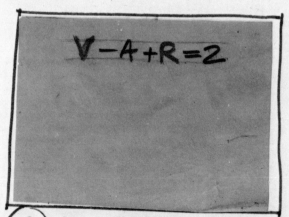

$$V - A + R = 2$$

⑫ MIX BACK TO BG.
AS ⑦ + BUMP ON
EQUATION.

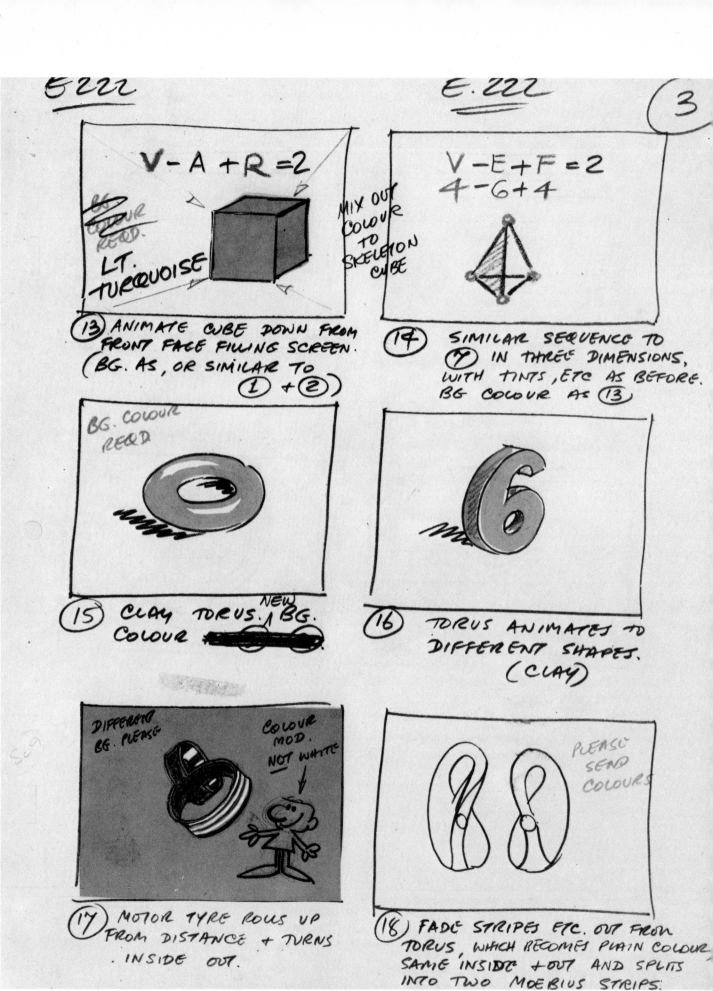

$$V - A + R = 2$$

LT. TURQUOISE

MIX OUT COLOUR TO SKELETON CUBE

⑬ ANIMATE CUBE DOWN FROM FRONT FACE FILLING SCREEN. (BG. AS, OR SIMILAR TO ① + ②)

$$V - E + F = 2$$
$$4 - 6 + 4$$

⑭ SIMILAR SEQUENCE TO ⑦ IN THREE DIMENSIONS, WITH TINTS, ETC AS BEFORE. BG COLOUR AS ⑬

BG. COLOUR REQD.

⑮ CLAY TORUS. BG. COLOUR

⑯ TORUS ANIMATES TO DIFFERENT SHAPES. (CLAY)

DIFFERENT BG. PLEASE

COLOUR MOD. NOT WHITE

⑰ MOTOR TYRE ROLLS UP FROM DISTANCE + TURNS INSIDE OUT.

PLEASE SEND COLOURS

⑱ FADE STRIPES ETC. OUT FROM TORUS, WHICH BECOMES PLAIN COLOUR SAME INSIDE + OUT AND SPLITS INTO TWO MOEBIUS STRIPS.

THE BEGINNING

When the story is just an idea and you are discussing it with the producer/director, make sure you write down the thoughts and comments as you go. You will find that time and time again you will end up with a slight variation of your original idea that has somehow or other become somebody else's idea!

Many people start right into the storyboard once the idea has been set down. I prefer to write an outline that states the objects and facts of the film first, otherwise you may find yourself with design problems in the middle of a storyboard, or solving technical problems by designing instead of writing (usually a more expensive way of doing it).

From your outline, add any illustrations that clarify points not self-evident.

Get comments at every stage. Keep adding and cutting material until you have a very rough storyboard that gives all the information of the film, but not necessarily the order of presentation of it.

If someone does not understand it, rewrite it until they do. *Do not* go into verbal explanations and say that it will be obvious in the film.

If you intend doing animation scriptwriting seriously, then you need some drawing ability, but a great deal can be done with drawing stencils, instant lettering, cut out photos from magazines, etc., anything that helps illustrate the points you have put down.

In any storyboard some facts will be easy to illustrate and others difficult. Start with the easy ones and see how far you can take them. You can often arrive at the difficult facts via them, and make them simpler to illustrate.

You may have the job of adapting a story from a book or comic. If you do, make sure you rethink the story in terms of film. Book symbolism came about because books are used in a certain way; films are used in a different way and should use symbols best expressed by film.

A FEW DOS AND DON'TS

Do not move anything that does not carry information. Move significant images in a way that is easily understood (e.g. it is better to slide a number from one part of the screen to another rather than pop it off and on again in a different place).

Do not give sound effects to anything that does not carry information. Make sure your effect is appropriate (a sound of footsteps off-screen approaching can anticipate the image and prepare the audience, but the sound of footsteps going off is usually an indulgence).

Do not use backgrounds or colour if they do not help define the information on the screen. Use backgrounds and colour where they help focus the significant part of the image.

Do not make sound effects compete with the commentary. Make sound effects complement the commentary by timing them to come during a natural pause in the commentary.

Do not suggest music on the track as a matter of routine. But suggest that music be used where it adds to the rhythm, movement and mood of the scene (especially when using music as sound effects).

Do not use the whole screen if you only need part of it. Mentally divide the screen up like a chessboard and give your important images the centre of the screen (the worst fault in most diagram films is to have busy movements in opposite corners that are difficult to relate together).

Do not use colour in a decorative sense if you intend to use it for colour coding symbols. Define distinct symbols in distinct colours, and make sure you keep it consistent throughout.

Do not jump from one scene to another or use too fast transitions. Leave a reference point as a shape, colour, movement, or sound and give the transition long enough to make the audience aware that it is a transition. (Your viewer's eye should not have to move very much from leaving the old image to seeing the new one).

Do not have key movement and a key word in the commentary coming on together. Repeat key words or movements where possible, and preferably make the commentary anticipate the movement.

Do not use reference points that date easily (fashion, jokes or slang terminology). Use reference points that have a clear identity with the audience you are aiming at (also use international symbols when there is a choice).

Do not use lip synchronisation unless it is absolutely necessary as it limits foreign translations, and focuses attention on the face when other movement could carry more information. Use lip sync if it is important to establish the personality of the main characters, or if the commentary carries all the information, and the film is not intended for foreign editions.

Do not make images conform to the laws of a real physical world if this is not essential to the story. Animation mainly deals with analogies. Treat the images as if you were thinking about them, and the screen portrays your thoughts.

Do make your film world consistent with itself. If you start lifelike characters, do not make them do uncharacteristic things half way through the film. A film has its own logic that must be kept.

FINISHING OFF

A storyboard may appear finished when it is not. The action and the words have been put together and seem to fit, but often the timing has not been worked out. It is not always clear in the storyboard whether an action precedes a word or a word precedes an action. To avoid bad timing, make separate pictures of one action, e.g.:

WORD SLIDES IN FAST. SCREECH TO A HALT.
WORD FLATTENS OUT TO SOUND OF CRASH
WORD BOUNCES BACK (BOING) INTO SHAPE.
COMMENTARY This word indicates......etc.

When you write the commentary underline the word where the action takes place. This is a guide to both animator and editor.

There may be a detailed drawing to go into the storyboard which is too complicated actually to put in.

This drawing should accompany the storyboard and a space be left for it (drawing) with the script and alongside the space.

If the space is for a live action clip that is to be inserted, make sure the timing is noted in the storyboard, e.g. Clip of moonshot (10 seconds). Also make sure that when clips are to be inserted, some provision is made for a transition from animation to the clip (mix, fade, wipe, etc.).

Sometimes a storyboard is finished but needs a scene that is unavailable. For example, I wanted to use a moonshot scene for one film, and included this in the storyboard, but later found I could not get the copyright. When this can possibly happen make sure you have an alternative scene to put in at the time of the storyboard being done. Do not wait until the storyboard goes into production and then find you have to do a hurried rewrite of that scene.

You may have done everything to make your storyboard clear, simple, entertaining, and factually correct. You feel pleased and so does everyone else, and the film goes into production. When it is finished and screened someone says that the film is now out of date. The scientific facts that were thought true three months ago have now been proved wrong (this has happened to me) the symbols you adopted are perfectly correct, but they are only used in America and the film is for world distribution (this also has happened to me).

Suppose the consultant approves the storyboard says everything is correct and will be valid for years.

You used his examples which he thought perfect; but he forgot to tell you that the examples he gave you were taken from his last book and he had sold the copyright. (Even this has happened to me).

A consultant is rarely a film maker. He will answer your questions truthfully, copyright questions, distribution questions, new discoveries, trends, and applications, that may affect your film are not his worry, they are yours. Make sure the consultant understands why you are making the film.

Where it is going to be shown. What purpose you expect it to fulfill. How long you expect the film to be valid, and then show the storyboard to at least one other expert in the same field just for comments.

HINTS AND SUGGESTIONS

Sometimes you will be landed with a very dull script to do a storyboard to. It may be very technical and not allow much freedom, or it may have been accepted and sponsored by someone who has little idea of films, and is not open to enlightenment. You have to make the best of it.

1. Make titles and end credits work to your advantage. If you can give a good opening and ending it is amazing how many people think they have seen a good film in between. An opening gag or colourful display should anticipate the subject and set the mood.

2. Use transitions (wipes, pans, mixes, fades, etc.) in an imaginative way. If you have to fade to black and fade on to white use a mix of several colours in between. It gives the audience time to digest what has gone before, and makes it very clear that a new scene is about to start.

3. If you have a static image like a map or technical diagram, and have to highlight parts of it, make full use of focusing methods for emphasis, or use a well designed and coloured arrow and give the arrow a personality (make it bend, wiggle, change colour or flash). Or put a ring round the area and give this some special effects. Alternatively use one of the following methods: ghost off the rest of the picture, zoom in on the key part, make the rest of the image become black and white, leaving colour only where it is informative, black out the rest of the image entirely, or give an enlarged version of this part in the corner of the screen while leaving the original image on screen. Vary these methods through the film.

In technical films, cycles like liquids flowing, electrons spinning and engines running, can become very boring. These can be given a better dramatic presentation by building up the cycle gradually as, for example, by showing a liquid flowing without the surrounding container. The container would then mix on complete, or part by part. Cycles can also be given interest with humourous sound effects, and sometimes making the cycle go wrong or in reverse when not expected. At no time should your audience be able to anticipate what is about to come. You should always be one step ahead of them.

Your most difficult information should be spaced throughout the film so that it does not become indigestible. A cycle can give the audience time to digest the preceding information.

If the subject matter is highly specialised and new to the audience make sure you have a common reference point to come back to after each new piece of information. If, for example, you are showing parts of the atom and going into sub-atomic particles, make sure the complete atom is referred to throughout and new information shown in its place. Going from one unknown to another is a very easy way to lose your audience.

If a film is to be shown a number of times, like cassette and loop films, do not use gags that only stand one showing.

Loop films can contain far more information than conventional films, especially if the projector can be stopped and each frame examined. But do not make such films into film-strips. Each frame should still lead onto the next, and not be considered separate from the scene as a whole.

If you are using analogies to describe processes, do not push the analogies too far. Ideally an analogy should only be adopted to describe one point in common.

Humour, like colour coding, should be used constructively. It is good to employ humour to make something go wrong and then show it going right. It is bad to bring in humour just because the situation is open to it. This can be an expensive indulgence. Even when humour is used constructively, it should not be contrived, but consistent with the logic of the film, and based upon the natural development of the storyline.

If you are writing for children, write from the standpoint of a child, do not write as an adult talking down to a child.

Animated film makers can learn a lot from the old silent comedies. It is a good test of a storyboard to see how much can be achieved without using sound.

EXPERIMENTAL FILMS

What is an experimental film?
1 One that develops a new technique like painting directly onto film.
2 One that develops a new style like the UPA break from Disney styling.
3 One that develops a new process like electronic special effects.
4 One that develops a new concept like cassette films, multi-screen, or computer animation.

Experimenting is exploring new territory but doing it methodically. It should be explainable, and to some extent justifiable. Flashing lights and making noises at random would not make an experimental film if there was no purpose behind it. Experiments of this type should not be imposed upon the public as they devalue the purpose of experimental films as a whole. A film maker who says that he is not interested in what the public thinks should not create a situation where they have to.

Unfortunately, a high proportion of experimental films have no purpose in that they do not lead anywhere.

How does one judge what leads where? There is one aspect of film that will always work however badly done—conviction. If a film maker is convinced that he has something to say, this will come across in the film. It will come across considerably stronger than the intellectual message that is well constructed, competently put over but lacks the emotional impact of conviction.

Probably the biggest trap to fall into is confusing the *art* of film with the *craft* of film. The art of film is knowing what it can do as a medium. Knowing how to use it to put over information in a way that exploits its special characteristics, and how to get the most out of these characteristics. The craft of film is knowing the mechanical and physical limitations of film equipment—film processes, studio routines, etc.

I have never met anyone who is an expert in both, and generally speaking, the artist who becomes a craftsman, no longer has anything to say.

Many people in animation have strong convictions about a subject but do not feel it is a subject for a film. They tend to wait for a 'great idea' to come along. When it does, the idea is usually related to something everyone is talking about, and the dozens of other film makers waiting for a great idea see it at the same time as you. How many times one has seen a flood of films, articles books, etc. on the same subject come out at the same time!

The golden rule is that if you *really* find something (anything) interesting then you can make others interested. The best ideas seem so obvious that they do not appear to need writing.

Perhaps you have an idea and feel that it can be developed but cannot see any leads. At this point inspiration is too long in coming so you approach it logically. For example, a man is walking through a park. He sees a flower. What does he do?

He tries to pick it but it refuses to be picked. He tries a number of methods, each of which fail.

He thinks it is the most beautiful thing in the world and builds a house round it. People visit the house. The house becomes more important than the flower.

He picks the flower to give to someone he loves, but she does not want the flower.

He plays a tune to the flower and it grows bigger and bigger.

He puts it in his buttonhole and starts a trend, etc. There are many developments from any situation.

The idea you have may not be the *beginning* of an idea, it may be the end. On the above theme work out some ideas on how he could end up with a flower. Does he collect them? Is he allergic to them? Does it symbolise something else?

Take the seed of your idea and see if it works in reverse. Change the man for a woman, make the ending the beginning, try adding or subtracting characters and see at what point it changes the storyline.

If a film has a general enough theme, various people will interpret it in different ways. This is good. If it makes sense on several levels then you have said something worth saying.

A good idea will sum up what most people know

already, but never clarified for themselves. It abstracts and defines a situation or set of events and simplifies them. Your idea may just be an area of interest with no defined focal point: women's liberation, teenage violence, pollution, religious experience, abuse of power, etc.

Discuss the subject of the idea with as many people as possible and note their comments. If opinions are divided about a subject, try to write a story illustrating both sides, such as teenage violence from a violent teenager's viewpoint as well as an adult's.

If the storyline still does not come, try to develop the main character. What does he represent? What sort of friends does he have? What goals and ambitions does he have in life? What does he love and hate most?

Then try presenting the story first as if the character did not know you were watching, then as if you were part of the scene, and then with him relating to you.

Jot down any idea that seems at all related to the story you want to tell, draw up any bits of the story as they occur to you even if the drawing does not lead anywhere. I have often found that once the first drawings go down, ideas follow quickly.

Chance will often turn up a good subject for a film. Some years ago I kept some magazine articles on the first computer animation, optical illusions, and the interpretation of doodles. I filed them away and forgot about them. When I was asked to devise some special effects, I checked through the file and found enough material and leads to develop several unexplored areas of animation. Anything that looks as if it can be animated should be kept. Sooner or later it will be.

Ideas come in cycles. They follow in the wake of new wars, new fashion trends, new scientific discoveries, etc.

The themes are often basically the same, and to some extent can be anticipated.

Do not be put off a subject because someone has done it before. Every subject worthy of comment will be done many times. If the comment is about an important subject like war or pollution then the more comments the better—provided you are attempting to give a clearer picture or a better answer to the situation.

No film is going to say everything about anything. You might well spend the rest of your life saying the same thing over and over again in different ways. If it is something you believe in, each statement will be a development of the last one. Set out to make each film say one thing clearly.

Every good idea will seem obvious in retrospect, and you will wonder why you did not think of it before. It is very probable that you did think of it before, you just did not write it down before. Ideas that are meaningful to you will occur over and over again in different ways. It is only when you write them down that you realise how often you have thought about them. When you have your good idea and have written it down, you should be able to explain the theme in one sentence. If you cannot do this then you have not worked it out enough.

If a writer in another field (books or live action films) has been able to say what you want to say, see if you can sum up his work or basic philosophy in one sentence.

If you can then you will have a source of ideas for a long time to come.

3. CARTOON STRIP TO ANIMATED FILM
Dusan Vukotic (Yugoslavia)

Dusan Vukotic has been one of the leading film makers in Yugoslavia since the late nineteen fifties. He won an Oscar with his film *Ersatz* in 1962 and, apart from working with animation he has made normal feature films and experimented with practically all elements of combined film technique.

He is one of those artists who insist on preparing their own story continuity and storyboard, and as a scriptwriter-director has a strict control of all creative processes in the production of his films.

On one occasion Hitchcock claimed that just one bizarre detail or some unusual situation occupied him to the extent that on this detail or, more precisely, around this detail, he was able to build his film. This way of working, which one should emphasize is an exception to the usual creative methods of scriptwriting for feature films, is however the unwritten rule. To work on a script for animated film involves the search for and creation of possibilities from the impossible but at the same time never forgetting that to be upside down and unusual is by itself not sufficient. If one has already decided upon scriptwriting for animation then the sooner one forgets all about the Aristotelian rules of drama and all the formulae of sophisticated illusionary drama the better. But if one must retain something then that could be the anti-illusionary elements of former theatre styles. Often while watching animated films a subconscious comparison with the comedy style of the Comedia dell'Arte has been impressed upon my mind. Drawn heroes, like the characters in the Comedia dell'Arte, "wear" permanent masks for permanent types. Harlequin, Bajazzo, Puccinella, Dottore, Capitano move with pantomime, acrobatics and use stylized humour. Scripts were very simple and usually everything took place around one situation which through the years successfully varied in this theatre of mask. And today, a Becket, a Pinter or an Ionesco employ the way of thinking which belongs to the anti-illusionary theatre in their so-called anti-drama. On film, Georges Méliès, Mack Sennett, Charlie Chaplin, the Marx Brothers, Jerry Lewis, to mention only a few, successfully convince us of the existence of the absurd. All of them use written or spoken words, actors, theatre and film technique but everything they cannot achieve is achieved by animation.

Animation is not burdened with the laws of physics. It is not enslaved to literal reality. It does not imitate life but interprets it. Because of that the first question I ask myself in connection with a script is—Could this text be shot with live actors without changing anything essential? If the reply is yes, this script is not suitable for animated film or, in other words, it is foolish to draw what may be filmed with actors.

In the case of a script for industrial, advertising or educational animated film, my discussion with the sponsor most often involves proving that the medium of animation has its specific language which is far more persuasive and expressive than a natural treatment. If the sponsor understands anything about animation the task of persuasion is not difficult. But where the reverse is the case the whole thing involves placing trust in the creator of the film. I shall give here one example which is not directly connected with animation but brilliantly illustrates the relation between author and sponsor.

On one occasion Bert Haanstra, the well-known Dutch documentary film maker told me about the creation of his film *Glass*, which won an Oscar. The sponsor had insisted on a pure industrial advertising film and he did not want to accept the director's suggestion for creating his own impression of the process of glass production. The only thing the director succeeded in obtaining from the producer was a greater length of film. Haanstra shot two films in parallel, one based on his own idea and the other according to the sponsor's wishes. Only when he saw both films on completion did the sponsor decide upon the Haanstra conception. The application of such a strategy is possible in the case of the live action film, but with animation this involves animating the same thing twice just to prove something to a stubborn sponsor. I, myself, would rather stay away from such a film.

The greatest number of misunderstandings about animated film occur when the purpose of the film is not precisely defined before the script is written. The sponsor or producer must know for whom they wish to design the film and this is the first specification necessary for scriptwriting. Animated film can be designed for children only, or for adults only, or for children and adults. An animated advertising spot should first and foremost communicate with the potential buyers of the product which is being advertised and not to all the viewers of TV programmes. Educational animated film must also be directed precisely because, for instance, Einstein's theory of relativity is presented in one way if the film is designed for the broad public whom we suppose do not have the faintest understanding of it, and in another way when the film is designed for physics students. Because of that the first question we ask the producer or sponsor, no matter what type of animated film we are dealing with, is for whom is it intended?

After completing discussions with the sponsor or producer the scriptwriter conducts a conversation with himself: "In the script shall I use a dialogue or accompanying spoken narration?". "Films with a dialogue are more difficult to place in foreign markets because to synchronise lip sync it is necessary to synchronise speaking parts with the language of the buying country, and this is more complicated and more expensive than translating a spoken narration.

"It is a good thing that the script is only based on animated drawing and music because for such film language barriers do not exist.

"But that is not always possible—it depends on the theme of the film.

Dusan Vukotic and
Boris Kolar

Full storyboard for a ten minute long
animated film *Piccolo*, which uses only
music and sound effects.

"I could throw in short written inserts as in the
silent films.

"This can hinder the rhythm of the film, and if
the film is intended for children then one must
take into account those children who have not yet
learned to read."

And so the monologue of the scriptwriter with
his dilemmas continues. Finally, it must be
decided for whom the film is intended and so help
the scriptwriter to choose the most suitable form
of scenario.

If I choose the script without a dialogue and
without accompanying spoken narration (I made
most of my own films in this way) I will use in the
script a text which describes only what is seen.
In other words, pure action.

Parallel to working on the basic idea I work out
in detail a series of rough drawings which should
suggest a visual side for the future film. Sometimes
the drawings are made after the text has been
written and sometimes the other way round. The
order is not important as it is only a question of

habit. But it is essential to have a continuous authentication of the possibilities between the text and the drawings. It very often happens that scriptwriters who start writing for animation are unable to express a written situation with drawings, because the drawing does not behave like a live actor and its scale of expression is completely different. "Drops of perspiration appeared on his forehead . . ." This scene is very easy to shoot with a live actor and with the help of glycerine, but the same scene when drawn is ridiculous, no matter how well it is animated. Physiology has no place in the world of animation. The real death of the drawing is not caused by loss of blood but by the rubber eraser. A stylized situation in animated film emphasises the strength of the expression whereas the realistic deadens it. The *raison d'etre* of the medium of animation is its autonomy and its own specific expression and not the imitation of other media.

During the first phase of the work when the basic idea is elaborated all the information must be

collected. This may be basically systematized according to three groups:

    A Contents—specific or general
    B Drawings
    C Sound

From experience I know that information conveyed by sound is most easily forgotten, but one can build comic and exciting dramatic effects with it. In my film *Piccolo,* I ascertained to what extent sound can be the prime mover in the film, a

functional originator of the whole movement and not only the sound background.

Briefly, the contents of the film are as follows:

Two friends live under the same roof and have the best of neighbourly relations. One day, one of them buys a small harmonica called Piccolo, and starts to play it. The monotonous playing soon becomes unbearable and the neighbour protests, but in vain. To gain revenge he buys a bigger instrument and very soon this develops into a playing contest between them. The neighbours

change their instruments, for others which will make a bigger and bigger noise. The sound of Piccolo is replaced by the violin, the sound of the violin is replaced by that of the contrabass, then comes the turn of the trumpet, then the drum, the piano, organ . . . and so on until the collapse of the house.

Many films have been made in which film makers have tried to visualise the sound; let us remember the interesting and worthwhile experiments of Len Lye and Norman McLaren.

Once all the data is gathered and systematised it requires selection. Overcrowding the content leads to a so-called "race against time" because the length of the film is usually decided in advance and into this allotted time the animator attempts to cram all that the scriptwriter wrote and the sponsor accepted. This often leads to vagueness because some scenes remain on the screen for too short a time.

Such obscurity causes the viewers to have to make an effort to follow the film, normal percep-

tion is not possible and therefore there is loss of interest in the further flow of action.

With the comparison of all the gathered information we necessarily have to select only a part of it. This is a phase we call compression. In the film of *Piccolo* the task of the introductory scene was to show in short the friendship and good relations between the main characters of the film.

Among the visual possibilities of showing friendship between two persons are the following:

1 They meet and greet each other by removing their hats.
2 They meet and cordially shake hands.
3 They meet and give each other friendly pats on the back.
4 They help each other in certain situations.
5 They exchange gifts.
6 Together they fend off the aggressive behaviour of a third party.
7 Etc. . . .

COMPARISON AND SELECTION

The first three solutions offered above are excluded because they are rather conventional and do not offer any special possibilities.

In the fourth and fifth solutions there exist potential animated film possibilities, which only require thorough elaboration.

We exclude the sixth solution because it calls for the introduction of a third personality who later becomes superfluous. After comparison and elaboration of the fourth and fifth solutions, we chose the fourth, which in the final conception looks like this:

Two windows open from a building. At the left window appears the shorter inhabitant—Small. At the right appears the taller inhabitant—Big.

Big puts a cigarette in his mouth and Small leans out of his window and kindly lights the other's cigarette. Then Small puts a pipe in his mouth, Big returning the favour by lighting his pipe. The

smoke from the cigarette and the pipe form two "halos" which hover over the heads of Big and Small.

It starts to rain. Small's flat leaks. Big skilfully climbs onto the roof and with a pair of scissors he "cuts" the rain above the roof of his neighbour. The leaking stops.

Beside Small's window is a tree in which a bird is singing. Big leans out of his window in order to see and hear the bird better. Small takes the tree with the bird and generously replants it beside

Big's window. The bird sings gaily.

(In the next sequence the melody which the bird is singing is taken over by the musical instrument and this time becomes fatal for the two friends).

If we analyse the previous situation we shall see a certain graduation:

1 The calm mutual lighting of cigarette and pipe.
2 "Halo" of smoke suggests the saintly characters of Big and Small.
3 The rain destroys the reinstated balance and

immediately after that an opening appears for the gag of "cutting" rain.

4 Generous presentation of the tree with the singing bird.

The sound of the rain in scene 3 suddenly stops and thus accentuates the appearance of the first important melody in the film interpretation—the bird's singing in scene 4.

We make a selection of information already gathered most often when we adapt a finished literary work. The scriptwriter tries to preserve the atmosphere and the spirit of the original work and to find adequate visual solutions for the verbal situation described. In 1958, I made a ten-minute animated film based on the novel *Vindicator* by Anton Chekhov. The beginning of the original novel is as follows:

A short time after he found his wife in the act of adultery, Fjodor Fjodorovich Sigajev stood in the weapon shop Schmux and Co. choosing a

suitable revolver. His face reflected anger, sorrow and unrecanted resoluteness. "I know what I have to do" he thought. "The family is disgraced, honour is stamped into the mud, sin triumphs and I, as a citizen and an honourable man, must be a vindicator. First I shall kill her and her lover, and then myself . . ."

He had not even chosen a revolver or killed anybody, but his imagination already drew three bloody corpses, fractured skulls, spattered brains, commotion, curious crowds, post mor-

tem . . . With the morbidity of a hurt man his mind dwelled upon the horror of his relatives and the public, the death-rattle of an unfaithful wife, and in his thoughts he already read the introductory articles discussing the destruction of the institution of the family.

The beginning of the script for animation is as follows:

Atmosphere of the period from the second half of the nineteenth century. The clerk Sigajev, completely withdrawn, hurries along the street.

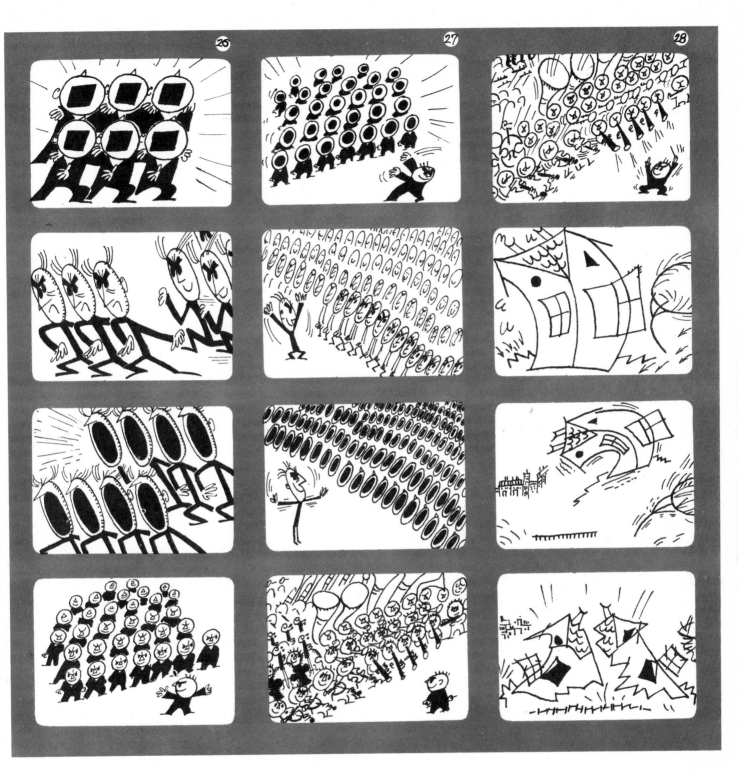

As he passes by a carriage he fawningly greets its occupant. Sigajev arrives at his house, takes the key and opens the door. In the corridor he pedantically removes his office coat. Further away a large framed family picture glares at him from the wall—he and his wife arm-in-arm, young and in the romantic presence of a silver birch tree.

From the bedroom comes a lascivious female laugh. Sigajev is surprised. On tiptoe he stealthily approaches the room and peeps through the keyhole. Beside the broad marital bed are his wife's slippers and next to them high, shiny officer's boots and sabre. The woman's laugh echoes again.

Contorted and in horror, the clerk Sigajev turns and looks in the direction of the wedding picture. His figure disappears from the picture and there, in its place, appears the seductive figure of the gallant officer. Sigajev smashes the picture. Under the smashed glass his figure appears once again beside his wife.

Out of his mind Sigajev runs along the street.

From somewhere in the distance comes his wife's piercing laugh.

The sign of the company Schmux & Co. In the shop window are different types of pistol. Sigajev rushes into the shop. He points to the pistols on the shelf.

The nimble, pot-bellied figure of the salesman demonstrates the weapon for Sigajev.

Sigajev takes the pistol and looks at it. The camera retreats from his face and now we can see Sigajev in his bedroom, pistol in hand. His wife, half-naked, screams.

The lover-officer protects her with his chest. Sigajev grins with the satisfaction of revenge. His red scarf floats in the wind like a victory flag. Sigajev shoots cold-bloodedly. He misses. His wife screams. The lover falls on his knees and begs for mercy.

Sigajev is merciless. The flame and bullet return to the barrel of the pistol. He shoots again.

The debauchees are punished. A meek smile on the clerk's face . . .

Comparing both texts, we see that the task of the scriptwriter was to change the first sentence from the novel, which only presents the fact that Sigajev's wife was unfaithful, into a visual affair. After that it was necessary to visualise Sigajev's monologue from the novel with the difference that for this scene much more information is given in the monologue itself.

THE VALUE OF SCENES

The continuous creative process unfurls in the mind of the script writer; imagination can be an inexhaustible source and because of that very often is more difficult to choose the right ideas and solutions than to invent new ones. Some scriptwriters for feature films very often use the method of a graph on which they mark the values of each scene. In such a way they attempt to analyse and control the values and rhythm of the scenes in the script. The scriptwriters of animated film have an advantage because such a graph perfectly replaces the script. The pictures are put in order and displayed on the wall of the workroom showing perfectly the "temperature" of the film. But not everything is achieved with action which goes logically and smoothly. A logically and smoothly related story can also be a boring story; and there is no worse criticism of an animated film than to say it makes one sleepy. Of course, that is not only related to comic film but also to lyric, poetic and dramatic film. What can we do to prevent that?

MAINTAINING INTEREST

If you have a script in which a bundle of dynamite explodes every minute, this is not enough because we live in an era of explosions and they are no longer interesting. If you believe in the magic formula of antagonism, then I advise you not to count too much on that, because we are also living in a period of co-existence. If you rely on five or six "exciting" chases in a script, then you are open to the accusation that you were bribed by the animators because they adore drawing in cycles (closed action). Finally, you collect or invent ten good jokes, then draw two figures, one telling the joke and the other listening and then the other telling a joke while the first listens. With five or six drawings you can successfully elaborate on a speaking mouth. Occasionally changing the position of the figure telling the joke makes the action more dynamic and requires only five or six new drawings. All that can be very successful and if someone by chance mentions that film is in the first place a visual art and that he could hear such jokes over the radio then he deserves to be called a hair-splitter.

Animation in all its forms is the art of movement and action.

Animation is not enslaved by any of the physical laws, not even by our usual conceptions of space, time and duration.

Animation can be burdened only by one's way of thinking.

Animation is a protest against the state of being static. One of the main problems for all scriptwriters is the problem of how to reinforce the theme at the correct moment and how to create intensive effects which are capable of retaining the attention and interest of the viewers during projection.

The notion of the "dramatic" appears not only in the film but also in literature, painting, sculpture, music, theatre and even in architecture. And because the art of animation to a certain extent synthesizes all these arts, it is always necessary to search for the scope to intensify all the components in an animated film.

STRENGTHENING THE THEME

A strengthening of the theme at the correct moment may be achieved in several ways:

A turning-point in the story content
Musical intervention
A drawn surprise
The use of colour
Contrapuntal sound (effects)
Camera movement

We usually find these ingredients combined in some degree or other. They must at least be elaborated and fixed in the script. The statement which we sometimes hear even today that it is not the work of the scriptwriter, but of the director of the film, is completely wrong.

Scenes which rely on the spectator's emotional involvement, the sentimental and soul-stirring ones, can contribute to the failure of a script, because while watching the film the spectator cannot identify with the object. Besides, someone who goes to see animated film expects in advance to witness something out of this world, he expects a meeting with the world of fiction and imagina-He is ready for allegory and unexpected crises and therefore a drop in intensity in an animated film is far more emphatic and for the spectator less tolerable, than that in the feature film. Let us now see some examples which show how scriptwriting treats illogical situations in animated film, and the misunderstandings which often occur.

Once, in our studio, the term "adventure of drawing" was in common use. It was a name for the experiments carried out by some of our scriptwriters and animators who were searching for all the possibilities of free movement and free behaviour in a drawn figure which was passing through a series of absurd and attractive situations—situations which were created just at will. On projection and when shown to the public the experiment was found to be unsuccessful. What was missing? The associative connection with some life experience. A metaphor or the most ordinary gag cannot exist by itself but must be related to something. If we want the absurd to have an effect on the spectator it must also have its plausible logic.

TIMING

A scriptwriter must also have a feeling for the specific time used in animated films, so-called "timing". The basic characteristic of timing is a reduction of time, about which the scriptwriter must take care whilst writing the script. It does not mean that he has to interfere with the timing of the animation itself, but he must suggest a mutual time relation of the sequences and their duration in the film as a whole.

Today, animation reduces time to a minimum. It is not concerned just with shortening time, but in finding the maximum expressiveness in this new dimension of duration. The real movement of a hand filmed as normal on 24 frames of a roll of film, but shortened to one half (12 frames), is not transposing live action into the domain of animated film. How should the movement be shortened, to what extent and in which form, to bring it to life in this new sense? This, the value of duration, is the problem which every animator must solve for himself in his individual way. Today, there is less need for the phasers, artists who insert the drawings between the extremes of movement, as the mechanical phases give way to freer drawings which each animator decides for himself without following any general rules. This is the essential difference between traditional and modern animated film. Each phase is created in the same way as the extreme. The modern animator is in effect, rather similar to the musical conductor: the phases are like notes—he knows what each represents but he can still animate it in many different ways.

For the rhythm of the film the so-called "still-stand" is very important. This is a completely static drawing showing a motionless figure on the screen. Previously such a state of affairs was unimaginable. Because of its static nature, it was considered to present too much of a contrast in its dynamic context. Today, it is very important means of forming the rhythm. Motionless drawing resists movement and automatically strengthens it.

ECONOMICS AND ARTISTIC SENSE

Reduced animation is however very often applied without invention or artistic responsibility purely for economic reasons. Unfortunately, today we meet an increasing number of such films in which the faces move only mechanically and the art of animation animates only the bodies of the characters. These are all practical considerations beyond any mystery which the science of animation might possess and each scriptwriter has to be, if nothing else, well informed about them.

But all these are only means to an end. In the first place there is, of course, the idea: we have to decide what to express and why exactly we chose animation to do it—no matter whether we apply it to moving drawings, objects, or pulsating lines produced by a computer.

I have worked on all types of animated films from short advertising spots to educational films and films with a free theme—so called entertainment films. With these last, I have often some initial feelings of insecurity. With sponsored films the discussion with the sponsor usually centres on a concrete theme, and one tries to find the most effective way of realising the theme successfully. Poetic freedom moves between the limits of the given task because any bigger change could destroy the intention of the film. For instance, in educational film, too many comic situations divert attention from the essential to the inessential.

Things are completely different with the sort of films where I can do as I want, from the beginning of the idea to the end of the film. The sheer scope of animation has often given me an initial feeling of insecurity—not knowing where or how to commence.

Just to create one scene I have thrown away hundreds of drawings. This was not because one drawing was better or worse than another, but because I always knew it could be different both in the structure and in the movement—in other words, in its life. Moreover, I have often had a feeling for the possible unity of past, present and future in the one moment, which animation offers. It is a question of the eternal dimension, because animation negates our visual ideas about space, time and duration.

Once, the great Czech master Jiri Trnka was telling me about the resistance of material—for example the material from which a puppet is made and in which it is dressed. We then drew a parallel with the animated cartoon where the conflict with materials does not exist but where the conflict with the idea does. They are obviously different qualities.

I have never had anything to do with a puppet film. I prefer the fight with the drawing and its poetic potential—the fight with the way of thinking or the metaphysical resistance of the idea, rather than the physical resistance of the real object. I believe that the movement starts for any real animator in himself and then, by means of the pen or brush, it is transposed on to paper. Often I used to try to find the necessary movement in my own subconscious movements, and even today I catch myself making some strange spontaneous gestures. Of course it has nothing to do with copying a grimace, but with trying to find more of life's expressive language. That is of great importance. It does not matter how abstract animation appears, the result is always based upon the experience of life itself.

Let us return to the script. We know that animation need not be applied only to drawing. Animation moves puppets, objects, photographs, light and shadow, different materials, sand, modelling clay. In a word it moves everything which in nature is static.

A particular script cannot be interpreted with equal success by all the techniques of animation, because the technique of writing a script itself depends on the method of animation to be used in the film. If we compare the animated cartoon, which is the oldest form of animation, with puppet films we shall see that these two genres are essentially different in rhythm. Dynamic and unfettered drawing is suited to a quick rhythm of movement and that gives the rhythm to the film itself. With puppet films, because of the nature of the puppets, the situation is the reverse. Also the possibilities for visual deformation and transformation which stress the action in drawings is much greater than that in puppet films. On the other hand, poetical timing in a puppet film is easier to accomplish than in the animated film. If, for any reason the scriptwriter requires the illusion of space, then the puppet film provides him with the scope for that more than the use of the multiplane camera in animated cartoon.

But the rule for the scriptwriter of live action films is also the rule for the writers of animated films—it is impossible to write successfully for all genres, because some things suit one person, and other things the other. It is good that it is like that because the geniuses are always somewhat under suspicion.

Finally, some advice. If somebody should make an animated film based on your script, do not get excited at the première of the film if it does not have very much connection with your original idea—that is just one of those things!

THE STORYTELLERS
PPROACH

ri Brdecka (Czechoslovakia)

Jiri Brdecka contributed to the writing of many animated and puppet films produced and directed by the late Jiri Trnka and Karel Zeman. He himself directed many outstanding animated films himself containing a great sense of humour and satire, among these films are "*The Letter M*", "*Plaisir D'Amour*", "*The Vengeance*", and "*Hunting in the Wood*". The latter contained a romantic visual style similar to that of "*Douanier Rousseau*" which was cleverly adapted for animation. His latest film "*The Miners' Rose*" is produced in the same graphic approach.

He is very much a part of the world famous Czech film industry and his contribution reveals his strong individuality which may not be acceptable or in the line of thinking of some readers. His reasoning about the function of a script however, arises from personal experience and can be considered as an attitude of someone who knows his business.

Apart from being a writer and director, Brdecka is an artist of considerable skill.

I make animated cartoons in a Prague studio belonging to a fairly large production company called Short Films. This organisation produces all our country's short films and animated cartoons regardless of length—so the name Short Films is not to be taken literally. In Prague Animated Cartoons Studio, directors work either as permanent employees on regular monthly salaries plus occasional overtime pay, or on a freelance basis with contracts for individual productions. Both these categories of person receive certain fees for the sale of author's rights and royalties for the showing of their films in cinemas and on television and for sale abroad. The number of permanent producers employed is substantially higher than the number of freelancers. It is worth noting that Jiri Trnka was always one of the latter, and guarded

his independence jealously. Gene Deitch, the American director who has been living in Prague for many years also works for the company. I have been employed as a permanent director for thirteen years.

The Czechoslovak animated cartoons studios (there are six altogether) make films for two types of customer. The former are Czechoslovak Film Distribution which provides the programmes for cinemas and Czechoslovak Film Export (FEX), responsible for exporting films to other countries. The latter group, one could say, are customers in the real sense of the word. They are either from our national television organisation, ministries, institutions, and clubs, or from abroad, and they back the film or in some cases do a co-production with our studios.

For the director and the scriptwriter both these categories of client Distribution & Export and the so-called real customers, create both advantages and disadvantages. Distribution and Export apart from the basic requirements, do not restrict the creative freedom of the makers. They view a finished film and either buy it or not. The second category of customer, both at home and abroad, naturally state their requirements beforehand. These, of course, create limitations but they are often readily accepted, because one earns far more on this type of film than the other. There is not the space for me to explain the reason for this difference in fees. It simply exists, and creates a certain tension between the two types of production.

As I have already mentioned, I am a permanent employee of the Prague Animated Cartoons Studios, where I direct my own scripts based usually on my own themes and subjects. I have only made two films that have been ordered by a customer. One was from abroad and very untypical, because I was given *carte blanche* for the work. Ninety per cent of my films are for Czechoslovak Distribution and Export. So I am not really qualified to talk about understanding or interpreting a sponsor's ideas, for instance. Though I do not deal directly with the sponsor, the thought of which would terrify me, I still have my studio producer to think of. He, of course, has the right to accept or refuse my theme and my script, to stop me during production and demand changes. This task is assigned partly to the executive producer, who is concerned only with the problems of budgeting. Then there is the "dramaturgist", which I believe is a purely Central European term, who is responsible for the artistic side and the idea of the script and the finished film. The producer is subordinate to the dramaturgist in question.

I am ultimately limited by and subordinate to others as is any other writer/director in any other social system, unless of course he is his own producer and censor. However, an experienced director who has achieved certain positive results and has gained a certain reputation with his

La Lettre 'M'
directed by
Jiri Brdecka.

producer, has a more advantageous position and greater creative freedom than the most talented beginner.

COLLABORATION WITH TRNKA

Between 1945 and 1957 I worked for Czechoslovak Animated Cartoons on a freelance basis, and then permanently. A most memorable period of my career was my script collaboration with Jiri Trnka. His thinking was outstandingly original, but produced not only positive but also negative results. It soon became clear to me that there was no other way but to subject myself to his thinking, to accept and respect it even if I did not agree with its process. So I became Trnka's sparring partner. This position did not exclude me from using my ideas in our collaboration, which was naturally formed and created in Trnka's spirit.

I had to forget my own preferences and succumb unconditionally to the services of Trnka's taste. Yet I am grateful for this unusual experience. Firstly, I realized what an enormous impact

cartoons can make, if of course they are the work of a talented and ambitious artist. With this in mind, Trnka knew what he had to say and often admitted that animated cartoons were his best way of saying it. He was also very style-conscious—not only of his style in writing and directing technique, but also in his fidelity to the spirit of the theme, which can so easily be betrayed. He never mentioned his most remarkable quality, possibly because of shyness, or because it was so natural to him that he took it for granted and never thought about it. I think this quality was the humanity and compassion in his work towards the underprivileged in society. This humanity was the life-giving breath that changed his lifeless puppets to beings of flesh and blood. And it was this that touched those who had reservations about his films or an aversion to animated cartoons altogether. Though Trnka gave me most of his scripts to read, I soon gave up asking him for the same service. I realized that if I took his advice I would probably make a better film than the one I had written, but certainly a different one. His mind could not look at someone else's material objectively. Therefore, I would never advise new writer/directors to seek advice from such a strong-minded individualist. Should they take such advice, they might find themselves on a very tempting path, but out of their depth and finally in such painful complications that they will perhaps be forced back to where they started. It is better to stumble along by yourself than with the help of someone who sees more penetratingly and differently from you.

I have made twenty films to date, most of them 300–400 metres (12 to 15 minutes). I always choose the theme myself and in most cases write the script.

I think my work is characteristic for its genre, themes, and for the graphic style of the cartoons. I have orientated myself towards work for the adult audience, except for two films intended for children. which I regret turned out badly.

I have never attempted the genre which made the animated cartoon famous. I mean what we in Czechoslovakia call "grotesque drawing" and in England is known as caricature. It rarely appears in animated cinematography.

THEMES AND INSPIRATION

Scriptwriting, of course, cannot be separated from that which precedes it—choice of theme! I have been lucky enough to be in the position to choose my own themes and, although I like to vary the content and form of my scripts, essentially I tell the same kind of story over and over again. My films include pure entertainment, social treatises, stories about historical inventions, ballads, philosophical parables, tales of horror and essays. In every case the style of the illustrations originated from the action of the story. Yet it is not always a story or an idea which inspires me to make a film. As every artist will confirm, it is sometimes simply an urge to create something which allows you to use your technical skill to the full. So here the inspiration comes from form and not content. So, in such a case I look for a story which can be simply used as a convenience as one uses a coat hanger or a picture hook. Let me give you an example.

Trnka and I were working on the script of *A Midsummer Night's Dream* and we came to the wedding feast which takes place in Theseus's Palace Gardens. An idea formed in my mind: an image of a formal, highly ornamental French park, which Puck transforms by magic into free and natural landscape. I suggested this effect to Trnka, but for some reason he rejected it and the idea stayed in reserve. What should be done with it? I felt that in that magic there was a baroque element which fascinated me, because for some time I had wanted to make a film which would evoke the splendours of baroque theatricality with its fairies, perspective decor, scenic wonders and ballets. Having found this, I was on the way, but I still needed a story. Though the idea originated from the realm of folklore as the old Beauty and the Beast theme does, with its evocative magic and setting the magical metamorphosis of the park which fascinated me could have the metamorphosis aspects of the park as pure narrative. In searching for it, I found an 18th century ideal for my scheme; reacting to Rationalism at this period gave birth to Romanticism, and the parks and chateaux, "laced with French corsets", acquired a new

La Lettre 'M' directed by Jiri Brdecka.

neighbour, the English Park, where nature was breathing freely and where gardeners' shears were prohibited. Both these parks along with their owners seemed to represent two aspects of human nature, Reason and Feeling. Here, then, I found the premise and key to the story: "Reason and Feeling" symbolised by two gardeners and their conflict and conciliation, followed by a combined effort to fuse their differences harmoniously. From then on the script was quite easy to write.

Naturally, this new vision dictated several changes. As I had chosen a pantomime-ballet form, music became an important aspect, and therefore the symbols of Reason and Feeling changed from gardeners to musicians and, in the final version, to dancers. I do not think it important that "Reason and Feeling", despite its high technical standard, did not live up to my expectations. I will give my reasons later. The film's short-comings were due, to a certain extent, to the writing.

I think that the way the graphic style influences the choice of theme is quite common in the field of animated cartoons. The graphic element plays a highly important role in this filmic form, so it is not surprising that this should be so. I have always chosen this procedure in my films, at the same time inventing a story which would at least appear as the principle idea.

Of course occasionally one finds a story which seems to have been written for an animated cartoon. Then you say to yourself: "This I must film!" and then go about choosing the most suitable designer for it. If an original idea for a theme occurs to you directly, then that is excellent. If, however, you get it secondhand or come across it in the pages of some book or magazine, it is worse because you run the risk of making illustrations rather than a proper animated cartoon film.

It is a great advantage if the author is familiar with the working problems involved. But say you make an accurate choice, and find a story which seems perfect. You tell yourself: "I will deduct a little here and add a little there and have a script ready for filming". Well, you will start filming, and do just that, and then start realizing the virtues of literary structure and its incompatibility with that of animated cartoons. If you choose a literary theme, then you must stick to the central idea and fundamental plot but at the same time adapt this plot to suit it to the medium of the cartoon.

A most successful film was *Gallina Fobelbirdae*. The Czech title was *A Badly Painted Hen*, the film script based on a book for children by Macourka. The original story tells of a teacher who asks his pupils to paint a hen. One of them, using his creative imagination, paints something not easily recognizable as a hen. The teacher, an unimaginative woman, ridicules him in front of the whole class. The boy's painting of the hen comes to life, not only as a work of art but literally and flies away.

It is caught by a famous ornithologist, who claims he has found a new and hitherto undiscovered species. He becomes very famous for his find and presents the hen to the zoo. There the teacher points it out enthusiastically to her pupils, not realizing that the creator of this famous bird stands in front of her. Although I knew Macourek's story, it began to absorb me only when I realized its potential as a means of showing two styles of visual art, one slavishly imitating nature and the other an imaginative and poetic kind which is art in the real sense of the word. For a thorough comparison, I thought it a good idea to introduce an opponent to my little hero, an unsympathetic pedant whom the teacher praises continually for having painted a hen, as she also sees it, with earthy realism. In my adaptation, I gave the boy-artist a little girl-friend who stands faithfully by his side despite all the derision. I made the ornithologist pedantic and scientifically ambitious, defined the teacher's character clearly and stressed the boy's poetic approach to reality and non-conformism.

To the drawings of the live hen and its strange existence, I have tried to give a bizarre and lyrical feeling. One could say that my adaptation acquired a more concrete and clearly defined result than Macourek's original. Yet if Macourek had used my procedure, it would not have served him well. The charm of his tale (not to mention the uniqueness of style; there is no punctuation) lies in the lightness, the sketchiness of the characters.

It is a literary soufflé. It would become too heavy if encumbered with the sort of details necessary in a film. If I had used this method, I would have produced a very watery film. Yes, literature is a dangerous ally for the film maker.

Of twenty films I have made, thirteen are mime, four are with commentary, and three with dialogue. In fact, one could describe them all as mimed because the characters never actually open their mouths to speak or sing. Most of my Czech colleagues use the same technique and the reasons for this non-synchronization are very simple. Czechoslovakia has language problems both internally and in relation to the rest of the world. To this I must add that Czechoslovakian film makers rely heavily on the export of cartoons. Dubbing is not a cheap affair, not even for foreign buyers. Commentary does not give too much trouble in this sphere and mime none at all. Pojar's excellent serial about two little bears made using silhouette puppets is actually also mime. The appeal of those witty and basically very sophisticated films, depends to a large degree on the spoken dialogue. Nevertheless, the puppets here do not open their mouths but only emphasise with gestures and mime the gist of the commentary. Though this is a solution by compromise and avoids the basic problems of dubbing, it does not prevent export difficulties.

I have given the technical reasons for using

mime in such cartoons. There is, however, another reason which to me is far more important. The cartoon appeals to our visual senses. Sound is a useful addition but should remain subservient to the visual. Sound or dialogue can overwhelm the visual element, slow down the action, and even reduce vision to simple illustration. I remember this happening in the Disney film *The Sword in the Stone*. During a long winded dialogue (like a filmed play) the animators had quite a job keeping the visuals alive and interesting. While I see a great purity of style in mimed cartoon films, I have to admit that those with talking characters have proved a great success with the public. I admire Disney's animators, who have used the style with real virtuosity. Nevertheless, just this production gave proof that the spoken word is like an ambitious genie; once let out of the bottle, he forgets his servitude, and becomes a tyrant.

Sometimes I think that I prefer the mime tech-nique simply to avoid certain technical difficulties entailed in the work of lip-sync dialogue. In any case I prefer mime because it defines the limits of my work. Limitation can be said to be the mother of invention. If, however, you give up the spoken word and achieve a certain success, no matter how cleverly you have avoided and how wittily you have replaced it with action, there is a danger when choosing material, that you will overestimate your abilities in that direction. Let me illustrate this point with an example from my screen adaptation of Gerald de Nerval's *The Bewitched Hand*, which I renamed *Revenge*.

The action takes place in Paris in the period of the Three Musketeers and tells a rather complicat-ed story of a kind young pate-maker, who is ridi-culed in front of his fiancée by a rowdy military officer. He knows that he can save his reputation only by a manly deed, a challenge to a duel. At the same time he is painfully aware of his physical

Storyboard for *The Miner's Rose* directed by Jiri Brdecka.

THE MINER'S ROSE
    Length: 9 mins.

(Space for instruction
  to animators including
  gestures and camera
  movements.)

(Instructions to
  Background
  Designer.)

Text of the lyric together with notes on the vocal interpretation and the timing of the song.

Detailed analysis of the coordination between music and picture as well as the overall timing of sequences.

weakness. In despair, he resorts to asking for help from a gypsy magician who casts a spell on his right hand. The gypsy does this for a price. He explicitly warns the pate-maker to pay up in time for this service, or it will be all the worse for him. The magic works perfectly; in the pate-maker's hand the sword pierces the formidable duellist like paper. However, the laws against duelling are strict and the unfortunate victor has proceedings hanging over his head, which makes him worry and forget to pay the gypsy. He succeeds in pacifying the official, but as he thanks him for the reprieve, his bewitched hand deals out an awful slap.

For this he is condemned to death and hanged. But the dead hand slaps the hangman and is cut off. The hand jumps off the gallows, causing great panic among the crowd, runs through the streets to the gypsy's house. It causes the gypsy's practice of black magic to be discovered. The gypsy is convicted and sent to the gallows.

Well, this classic horror story is written in the spirit of black comedy by a half-mad French Romantic. I do not have to over-emphasise the great suitability of a bewitched hand as ideal subject matter for the animator. The hand, once cut off by the hangman's axe, develops its own life, and moves and jumps horribly. Moreover, I was tempted by the twilight atmosphere of the story, set in the period of the fantastical knight Callot, a favourite of the Romantics.

This story by Nerval was as if destined to be expressed by illustration. In short, I was inspired again by obvious pictorial possibilities. No sooner had I started to write the script than I realised what difficulties awaited me if I kept to the usual style of mime.

Although the literary original that I had chosen was full of action, nevertheless dialogue played an important part and even imparted important information. I had, therefore, to make a big effort to illustrate the meaning of the dialogue in a roundabout way, pictorially. I found my finished script complex and long winded because of this elaborate process. Now I realize that a few words of commentary or a suitable caption would have saved me a lot of unnecessary work and spared the audience that extra effort in following.

Purity in form, though praiseworthy, must not be allowed to destroy the impact of the original story. If there is a risk of this, orthodoxy must give way to compromise. Trnka, a confirmed enemy of such concessions, had to pay for his high principles on many occasions. *A Midsummer Night's Dream* was shown in Czechoslovak cinemas with a commentary added against his wishes, and as far as I remember, the same happened with the export version of *The Emperor's Nightingale*. What can be more annoying than such additions (never intended by the maker) injuring the spectator's sensitivity like a splinter under the nail.

RESCRIPTING STAGE

For me, scripting the film is the most tedious part of my work. One could compare it with seeing your route only on a map, and yearning to see the scenery and to have the experience of direct contact. This process is all the more unreal as it does not lead through reality but through a mirage which will only become concrete once production is complete. When I sit down with a sheet of paper, I have in mind only the main points on which to build the outline of the story. Very rarely does a "treatment" precede this work, which I avoid not out of laziness but out of an inability to write two or three pages of outline. I am incapable of thinking in generalities. My brain works better when I link one detail to another, thus unwinding a chain of ideas each originating from its predecessor. Of course, you have to alternate between invention and an objective viewpoint which determines the structural proportions of the plot. It is true that sometimes my mind gets carried away with minute detail, perfect for good animation but harmful to narrative structure. Such defects, if I notice them are thrown out in the next stage, that is while making the picture storyboard. In the script I note the technical instructions, such as the pattern and quality of the shots and camera movement, which are revised in making the picture storyboard. It goes without saying that much of what is written is changed in production and in the final editing. These corrections, however, concern only the details.

While working in animated cartoon films I have come to realize that I am more a script writer who directs than a director who writes his own scripts. I have already mentioned the pleasure I get from writing the stories. Quite frankly, the filming is less enjoyable. Regretfully, when these ideas become concrete and real, they only partly live up to my concept. When directing, I always feel my limitations in camera tricks and laboratory technique. I simply do not have the talent for these things, or perhaps one could say I have a highly developed anti-talent. That does not mean I do not like technical tricks. On the contrary, when I see films abundant with them at festivals, I get green with envy. I imagine I could never achieve anything like them, even with the help of the very best equipment, because I could not think up a script that could exploit these filmic miracles. I have always admired Trnka, because he picked up new techniques very quickly and could make good use of them. Karel Zeman, the great film magician, would often begin with a technical idea and then script a story around it. In this case the "How" has first place and the "What" only the second.

If, while writing the script, any directional details occur to me, I jot down as many of the details as possible. Yet I am not sure if this is a good method. I use it because it suits my type of detailed thinking. I realise that such a minutely worked out script can be a danger to a director. Every film begins to live its own life when shooting starts. When you sit in the projection room or at the editing machine, you feel new aspects crop up, new possibilities inspired by the visual impression of the shots and sequences. It is not surprising because even the most carefully thought out pages of the most happily inspired script are only theory. They may not work out in production. I often find this when I am directing. I have great difficulty in discarding a beautifully planned, carefully written idea, which in truth works well only on the written page.

The best writing method is the one that leaves the way open for the director to improvise. Naturally, the improvisation must respect the plot and style. One would think that I would practice what I preach. Unfortunately, after thirteen years of working the wrong way, I cannot change. There is a saying in Czech: "Habit is an iron shirt".

From time to time I brood over those unsuccessful films of mine which had promising scripts. The reasons for failure vary. The more subtle they are the more interesting. A good example is *Reason and Emotion* which I have already talked about, and from which I and the studio expected so much. It was an allegory, about the conflict between Reason (a serious trumpeter) and Feeling (a frivolous Piccolo player). Each tried to inflict his ideas on the other and then ended making it up and collaborating.

The illustrators did their best, colours were radiant, the music thundered, and the result? An honourable wreck, a wreck nevertheless. When I see *Reason and Emotion* today, after a ten year interval, I see the mistakes as clearly as the palm of my hand. I realize I wrote the script very conscientiously, but in a stilted way. In writing it, I used reason and not emotion. The main cause of its failure, however, was the choice of the designer who, despite his excellence, had the wrong style for this film. Zdenek Seydl, uses abstract forms or, in other words, has a non-naturalistic style. He is purely decorative artist who distorts realism with constant stylization, resembling an abstract ornament foreshadowing psychedelic art by ten of fifteen years. I think this description is enough to explain the reasons for our incompatibility in working on a theme which, after all, had Nature as its core.

Perhaps this example should not be quoted in a book which deals specifically with the problems of writing the scenario for animated cartoons. Nevertheless, anyone slightly aquainted with the business realizes that not only the script, but the mere theme should suggest a certain style to the director.

Perhaps I am not saying anything new to those who are directors and designers of their own cartoons. Of course, this is not so in my own case. During thirteen years, I have worked with about fourteen designers and, if I continue making cartoons, their number will certainly increase. The graphic element of film cartoon making becomes more and more important to me. When I started directing, because of inexperience, I considered it a servant. Today, I consider the graphic element an equal partner and sometimes the master.

5. THE ADVERTISING MESSAGE

Samuel Magdoff (U.S.A.)

Samuel Magdoff, formerly a producer of television commercials in the USA, reveals the care and concern which accompanies even the shortest animated film for advertising.

Visual scripting is an essential function in advertising film. The production cost for a half minute commercial could be higher than for a ten minute educational film. The production must leave very little to chance. For this reason the cost of a storyboard is also expensive. It is usual that a specialised scriptwriter works together with a visualiser within the agency itself in order to make sure from the agency's point of view that the advertising message should satisfy the client. Too often the copywriter also contributes to the text with lines which do not lend easily to the visual medium.

The best method however is a co-ordinated approach between the scriptwriter from the agency, an expert storyboard artist and the producer of the actual film.

Apart from the functional aspect of preproduction visualisation, the advertising industry has the additional problem of presenting a project to a client for the obvious reasons of impressing him. It is usual therefore to produce two storyboards, one to create an impact, the other to create the actual film. The two seldom mix—it is in fact customary to employ an agency trained artist for the first while the other is completely functional from the technical point of view.

These problems are revealed by Mr. Magdoff with illustrations from well known commercials.

The television commercial has become an art form all its own. Its goal is to motivate the viewer to do something or to buy something or, less frequently, to change his mind about a candidate or an issue. This task must be achieved within the limitations imposed by the client and his product, and within the dimensions, in time, of sixty seconds, in space, of a few square inches of television screen. We do the job with great commercial success—and, frequently, with good taste, sensitivity, and imagination.

Conceiving, writing, creating storyboards, and producing these mini-movies for television is a highly specialised art. For the writer, it poses problems very different from those confronting him in other media.

You will see that this contraption ... will make a revolution in our life—in the life of writers. It is a direct attack on the old methods of literary art. We shall have to adapt ourselves to the shadowy screen and the cold machine. A new form of writing will be necessary. I have thought of that and I can feel what is coming.

But I rather like it. This swift change of scene, this blending of emotion and experience—it is much better than the heavy, long drawn-out writing to which we are accustomed. It is closer to life. In life, too, changes and transitions flash before our eyes, and emotions of the soul are like a hurricane. The cinema has divined the mystery of motion. And that is greatness.

Actually, that was not said about television, or commercials (although I think it would have been appropriate), it was said about the movies—and it was written in 1908, by Leo Tolstoy. The remarkable thing is that he was aware, even then, that this new form of communication—one that is now so much a part of our lives—would require a special kind of writing.

A dog says neither "woof" nor "arf"; a brook does not really burble, or gurgle, or babble; in reality, they make other sounds. In this case, words are used simply as onomatopoeic symbols, close in meaning and sound to what they represent but not the real thing. In a film, we can "say" the real thing by using sound-effects. And we can "say" a lot more. When you say "chair", what do you mean? A barber's chair? An electric chair? An African camp chair? A director's chair? In film, we can avoid ambiguity by showing the specific object: here, the particular chair we have in mind.

Frequently, the first thing to be deleted from a film is the words. And that, as far as I am concerned, is probably the key difference between traditional "writing" and "visual writing". For thousands of years our basic means of communication has been through words. Film and television communicate differently. The gesture, the image, the action you see is dominating and the more memorable element in this new medium. Actually we say it is new, and we say it is sophisticated, but aspects of this "new" communication date from prehistoric times:

Gesture language is commonly conceded to have preceded oral speech, some say by at least one million years. It is further estimated that some seven hundred thousand distinct elementary gestures can be produced by facial expressions, postures, movements of the arms, wrists, fingers, etc., and their combinations.

This is not from a manual for animators: rather, it is a trenchant comment from *The Story of Language* by Mario Pei.

A live film, rather than an animated illustration, of what I am talking about began with a 30-page script. The final film contains not one spoken word; the visuals tell the story so cogently that words are not needed. However, it is not merely the stringing together of graphically eye-catching episodes that makes the film exciting. For one thing, it was carefully edited to a driving score created by Jazzman Chico Hamilton, since the intended use of this film was as the audio-visual portion of a display. But its career did not stop there. It was first released as a short subject and played in most of the art movie houses in the U.S.A Then it was adopted by the USIA and displayed around the world as part of their graphics art exhibitions.

nuel Magdoff

ryboards from six commercials
Electra Film Company—New York.
fortunately, this organisation is no
ger operational. The great varia-
ns of the advertising market forces
ducers and animators to constant
rouping.

istmas Birds

storyboard designed by Robert
chman for C.B.S. Christmas
etings. Originality, humour and
plicity are typical of the cartoonist
chman's work.

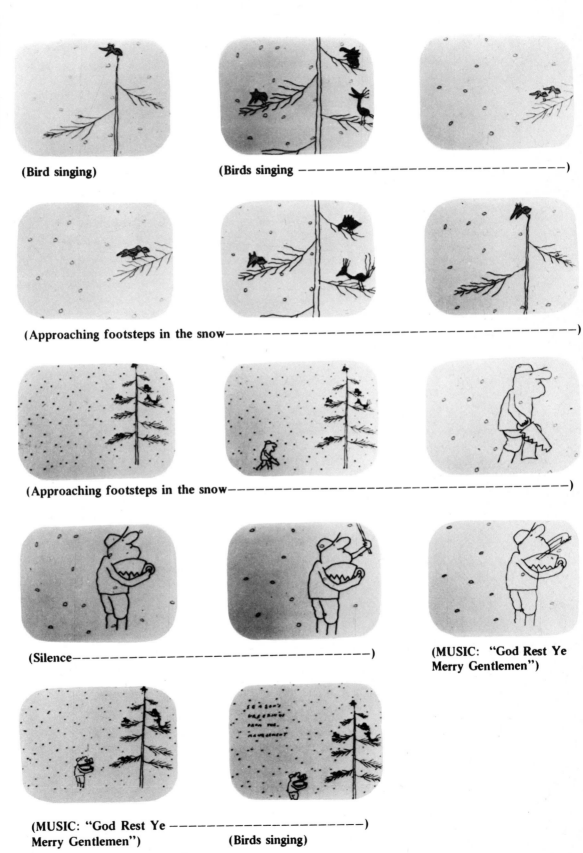

(Bird singing)   (Birds singing —————————————————————)

(Approaching footsteps in the snow————————————————————————)

(Approaching footsteps in the snow———————————————————————)

(Silence—————————————————————)   (MUSIC: "God Rest Ye Merry Gentlemen")

(MUSIC: "God Rest Ye Merry Gentlemen")   (Birds singing)

Final character designs for *Sheer Indulgence.*

54

(SILENT)

(SILENT)

(SILENT)

NNCR: A woman can indulge
erself in a thousand ways these days.

What with lotions and potions,
and ruffles and frills, . . .

and hair in this length, and that
color.

belt here, a scarf there.

Minis and bell-bottom trousers.

But for indulging your legs, only one
way remains . . .

(SILENT)

Hanes.

(SILENT)

Character styling for the commercial.

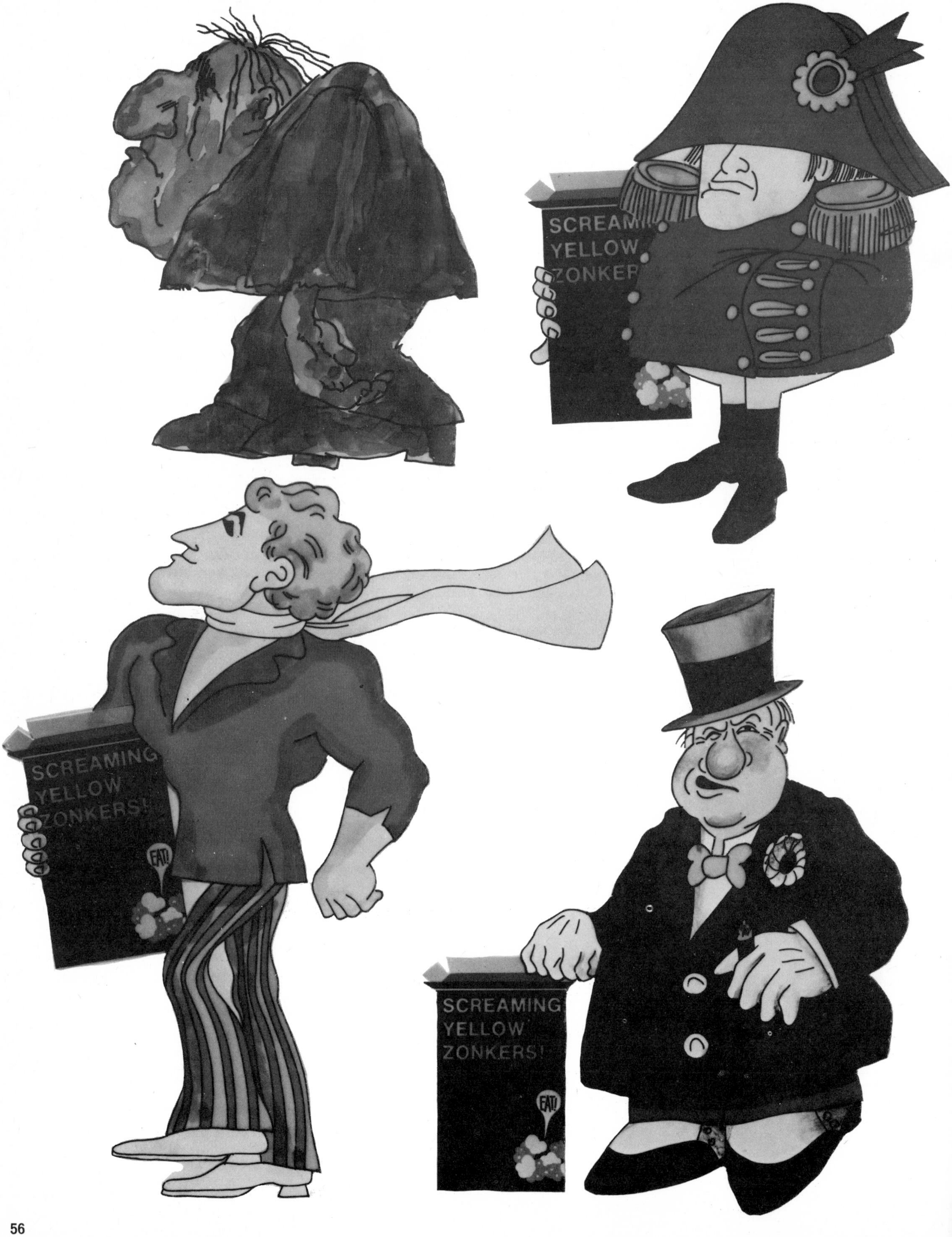

Zonkers storyboard.

ANNCR: Once there existed, an ugly, ugly person.

And what made him so ugly was that he had no taste, not one.

One day he stumbled upon a box of Screaming Yellow Zonkers and stuffed some into his face.

Well, to his astoundment they was great.

Wait, they were more than great. They was a magical, butter glaze popcorn snack.

So if you're ugly . . .

or even semi-rotten looking . . .

Try Zonkers.

Maybe they'll change your life.

(SILENT)

Maybe not.

HEAD IS
2/3 OF HEIGHT

GROG

CAN'T SPEAK, BUT TRIES
TO SAY WORDS!

WILEY

IS A SUPERSTIOUS POET, AND
SOMGTIME BASEBALL MANAGER!
HAS A TERRIFIC FEAR OF WATER
AND WORDS BEGINNING WITH "W".

(SILENT)

THOR: Hi Wiley. Fill'er up with Marathon Super "M."

WILEY: Ya wanna pull'er up a bit more?

(SILENT)

WILEY: Here's one of our new B.C. glasses, sir.

THOR: Thanks. Just put it in the trunk.

ANNCR: Get your new B.C. glasses free at Marathon . . .

where all petroleum products and automotive services are guaranteed in writing ...satisfaction or your money back.

Ask about the deal on a matching B.C. pitcher.

Final artwork
from *Nervin* commercial.

BAND: Hello Gloria, I'm
e . . .

Gloria what's wrong? You don't
seem yourself.

WIFE: Everything is wrong . . . I'm
just a bundle of nerves. The postage
is due . . .

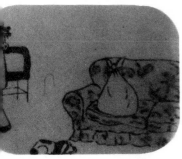

NCR: Miles' Nervine is a
xer for simple nervous
ion.

Take Nervine as directed during
a tense day . . .

and chances are you won't be a
bundle of nerves by the end of it.

(SILENT)

WIFE: Elliot, it's me again.

HUSBAND: God . . . lets eat.

(SILENT)

61

(SILENT)

ANNCR: (VO) When King
Charles visited the Globe . . .

every Orange Girl in the theatre . . .

ried unsuccessfully to sell him
er wares.

Then Nell Gwyn Whitehead
kinswoman of Schweppes'
Commander- . . .

Came on with whole orange bit-
including peel . . .

rom some of her Bitter Orange
rink . . .

which was so sensational . . .

she made it to the palace that night.

(SILENT)

TEAM PRODUCT

"Did you write this?" I asked a young man who was in the screening room a few months ago during the showing of a commercial. He looked at me very carefully and replied "Only the words". The young man did not intend to be funny. He was really being honest. He was just describing exactly what he had done. He had written the words, somebody else had drawn the pictures, and many others had been responsible for the total production. As he saw it, his entire contribution to the finished commercial had been "only the words". In point of fact, the current trend is away from rigidly circumscribed roles and toward group creativity.

Commercials, unlike paintings or novels or sculpture, are not created by individuals but by teams. Of course, every commercial starts with an idea. When someone in a meeting jumps up and says "I've got it" or when someone comes in with scribbles on the back of an envelope, and it is good, you sense it immediately. You feel something physically when you hear a good idea. The excitement does not stop there; that is only the beginning. The impetus of creativity continues—from script, through storyboard, through design, layout, animation, soundtrack, music; the whole gestalt, the entire process—is impelled by creative decisions. Whether it is sound effects, a change in the pencil test or the colour of the answer print, creative decisions are made until the moment the commercial is on the air.

The more cohesive the production team, the more closely they can work together, the better the commercial. It is not at all unusual to have a dozen or so very talented people working on one 30- or 60-second film. The writers, the animators, the art directors, the "guest" cartoonists, and the musicians are often among the finest in the world. The ideas have been excellent to start with, and everyone involved in the production has been able to change, adapt, and make concessions to the others to achieve the best possible film.

The following films are my personal favourites. Their production was the result of well-integrated teamwork, but the notion of group creativity predated that phase of their development. The films were all originated, conceived, or written by one of three different processes. The creator was a cartoonist who was also a writer, or a writer who was also a cartoonist or an illustrator, or (and this seems to be the trend), a writer-art director whose work is so tightly interwoven that it is often impossible to locate the germination point of the idea. Sometimes the words came first, sometimes the pictures. The important thing is that the blend is such a beautiful combination of thought and picture that the resulting commercial does what it sets out to do—convince someone, sell someone, make the viewer aware of a product or idea that may be novel to him.

CHRISTMAS BIRDS

My colleague and friend, Bob Blechman, was sitting in a movie theatre one day when an art card came on screen. It read: "Season's Greetings from the Management". It was pretty awful, and he speculated that it might be nice if there were something pleasant and a little more tasteful to be flashed on the screen and remain in keeping with the season. *Christmas Birds* was the result. It is actually one of Bob's own Christmas cards that has been animated. The illustrations show the original card and then the photoboard of the actual spot.

In this film, again, there is no narration, just music. The sound track "speaks" far more eloquently than words could. It is an unusual example of commercial animation, because there was no client and no product to "sell".

HANES BIRD

The Hanes script was one of the most sophisticated we have ever seen or worked with. In one paragraph, the creator completely described the concept, action, mood, and feeling he wanted. The "problem" was to adhere as closely to the original concept as possible and not go off at a tangent. Here is the description:

"A small, plain bird dresses itself. First, a beautiful big macaw-like beak. Then, a huge ring of colour around its eyes. A magnificent tailpiece. A plumed headpiece. A brilliant coat of feathers. Finally, it wriggles its short legs into a pair of pantyhose, during which the legs grow longer and longer. Completely dressed, it strikes a fashion pose."

Such a clear description meant we were able to follow the original idea exactly at all stages of production. Commercially, this bird is a little different from the Blechman birds—there was a product to sell and a client to foot the bill.

MARATHON

This campaign is excellent as an example of a successful group effort. At times the production resembled the more gruelling aspects of group therapy. Not only did the agency have to work with the original client—Johnny Hart, the creator of the BC characters. He insisted upon strict adherence to his comic-strip creations. With the agency, he shared approval of script, storyboards, continuity boards, sound tracks, pencil tests, and answer prints. His characters had never been animated before, so they never really had "voices". If you want to have fun one day, try picking a voice for an ant. Then try to get approval of the creator, and then the approval of your client.

Besides being an extraordinary campaign, this series is mentioned for several different reasons.

First of all, it utilizes already-established cartoon characters. And, with few embellishments other than movement and sound, these characters turned out to be effective salesmen. We maintained the integrity of the characters' personalities; if these had been lost, the campaign would have had a phoney ring. Result—no sale.

SCHWEPPES

Here is a perfect example of a print campaign that followed television's major thrust. Schweppes ran full-page ads in a comic-strip or storyboard form designed by the same man who designed the television commercials.

The story line and the graphic style, in turn, helped guide the hand of the animators to develop an appropriate approach to character movement to tell the story in the most dramatic way.

The concept, the design of the characters, and the narration called for a stylized technique. To point up the stylized movement, the characters occasionally slip in to ways of moving that imitate life. The moments of lifelike movement are a subtle counterpoint to the rigorous stylization seen during most of the film, and enhance the viewer's pleasure in its unreality. The juxtaposition of opposing techniques is also a key ingredient in humour. One always hopes that the injection of "life" will raise the level of an already funny spot to a more full-bodied sort of humour.

NERVINE

A Nervine commercial we produced may be a good example of a product seeking a very specific audience or population of potential buyers. Nervine is a proprietary drug to calm the nerves. The target audience is the harassed, more urban middle-class type. The "nerve wracked" reader of the *New Yorker* magazine, maybe? (William Steig, "New Yorker" cartoonist was the designer of the characters).

Plays are frequently written for specific actors to perform; this commercial was written with a cast of Steigian characters in mind. The narration

by the cast of live actors is in perfect harmony with the visuals, making the fantasy world come to life. What has been achieved is a soothing combination—a most effective selling tool that is also an artistic achievement.

SCREAMING YELLOW ZONKERS

This is probably the wildest campaign we have ever worked on. It originated with the startling idea of creating a black package.

Here is an example of what the package says:

"What to do with Screaming Yellow Zonkers! Put them in your mouth. Put them in your friend's mouth. Read to them. Dress them up and take them to the show. Tease them. Yell back at them. Iron them."

The first package (and you'll be sure there'll be many more) has a "Win a Continent Contest." If you recognize the mystery voice no later than 1947, you may win the continent of your choice.

The commercials, like the package, are offbeat. There is very little story line; they are more like a series of one-liners and blackouts. Peculiar things happen in them. For example, a monster keeps metamorphosing into something less monstrous as he continues to eat his Screaming Yellow Zonkers. Animation is the ideal technique to effect such an unlikely transformation—it makes the implausible inevitable and, in this case, the impossible profitable.

The stakes in commercials are very high. The profits to the advertisers from a successful commercial are often staggering. The power and effectiveness of the short film-form is shown time and again by mounting sales. It is no wonder, then, that the quantity of money poured into 60 seconds should be proportionately greater than for any other type of film.

Many of the techniques created and exploited in commercials find their way into other areas of the film industry; the most obvious being in the field of preschool education. The highly successful TV series *Sesame Street*, directly applies the technique and methodology developed for TV commercials to its own advantage.

6. PAINTER AND THE MOVING PICTURE

Ernest & Giselle Ansorge
(Switzerland)

Ernest and Giselle Ansorge's films *The Ravens* and *Fantasmatic* are recognised as masterpieces in their particular approach of graphic animation.

Mr. Ansorge maintains that since their films do not include commentary and are purely based on visual continuity, it is sufficient for them to start production from a carefully prepared storyboard.

The timing and continuity therefore are arranged during the production of the storyboard and the process of the production takes careful guidance from this without losing spontaneity during production.

The actual shooting of the films is carried out manually by the two artists themselves. They use cut out figures which are manipulated frame by frame to a musical guide, and make adjustments to the characters as they go along. They feel that in this way they are able to adopt an individual attitude to the work as it progresses, as well as maintain sufficient inspiration and it is easy for them if they want to make some alterations. They do understand the risks involved and admit that such a procedure is only possible with an individual unit working on its own.

SCRIPTWRITING FOR ANIMATION

It is as hard to define a method for scriptwriting as it is to write a script. Besides, does any one method exist? There is none of absolute value, for if there were, it would be possible to mass produce works of art.

Perfect as it might be, no piece of work can do without that personal touch which reflects the sensibility of its author. The important thing to me, is just this little piece of individuality which is destined to be shared with the spectator. It is here that the artistic emotion passes into the work.

Trying not to generalise, I shall draw on my personal experience to make a few remarks about the production of an experimental film, which I would rather term "free inspiration film".

This presupposes a complete freedom, with no restrictions other than those conerning finance for the film, which is of course a restriction.

My first definition would be: Use of the method which is appropriate to the subject of the film and to its nature: *animation*.

To create a work of art, one can use all materials in existence: wood, earth, metal, string, etc. but we must respect these materials and use them in the proper way. It would be wrong to make a mosaic by painting a pseudo-mosaic on marble, to smelt a statue in plastic to imitate bronze etc.

I think we can establish a parallel in the cinema: the *animation cinema* was invented for the creation of films which could not be made in live action, or to illustrate a story which must be suggested rather than told.

My definition of a good animated film is one which cannot be retold, cannot be summarised but has to be seen.

The frame-by-frame cinema has created its own specific language. I can do no better than to quote André Martin:

"In both recreating and seeking the self, animation, the cinema of total creation, offers us opportunities for infinite broadening of the formal setting of the animated image. It is absolutely necessary for the men of pictures in a happy era to dare to use, without reticence, a supple and a free visual language, capable of coping with the enormous diversity of visions, sensibilities and styles, lending itself equally well to the recreation of wonders of fantasy and of miracle as to the expression of the inimitable strangeness of the interior landscape."

Once one has found the basic idea, that is, the main subject, it has to be developed, given depth, made to re-echo, to be framed in a graphic style suited to its function, given a rhythm and a progression, both on the formal and the intellectual plane, and its impact must be prolonged by means of a soundtrack which is firmly implanted in the subject matter.

VISUAL DELIRIUM

Because of its infinite possibilities the animated film opens up the lock-gates of the director's imagination, and this brings the first danger: uncontrolled visual delirium.

We must not forget, right from the beginning, this neat little idea which is in your mind. It must not be dragged in all directions with a great fuss and commotion only to produce a superb firework.

The animation cinema is first and foremost the cinema of the mind. It passes through the creator's brain before reaching the artist's hand. It must not be reduced to a few brilliant pencil-strokes. It is above all a polemical and a reflective instrument, and it does not fear to look into the future.

For this reason, from among a welter of ideas, it is important to single out the one essential idea which will give the film its tone and its unity.

During the course of these considerations I do not exclude the gag film, which may be trenchant and educational. Just one good gag which is sustained and well developed seems to me to be superior to a succession of gags with no apparent link.

When the outline has been decided and the writer's idea has been well considered by the director, we may now pass on to the choice of technical means.

There are no *a priori* rules governing this choice. I can only say that I personally prefer drawing directly on to the cell for a gag film, but cut or torn paper silhouettes for films of more naive inspiration (films for children), dolls for folk-inspired films, the engraving style for certain subjects which require more atmosphere. All these methods have been brilliantly illustrated by animators in different countries of the world.

I used texturised animation for many of my films (*Les Corbeaux, Fantasmatic, Alunissons*), because this process suits me, and represents the graphic form corresponding to what I would like to say. The same idea could be expressed on cells or by means of a different technique and using a different artist. Each has his own inclinations.

FALSE ENDINGS

In all films there is one essential sequence. It comes near the end and this certainly is the *bete noire* of film makers generally.

It might occur to the creator right at the beginning, at the same time as the choice of subject. But, unfortunately, not always. How frequently a film in effect, ends before its intended climax because the author was unable to provide the "star" sequence! If you have not found a real ending, false endings are multiplied, which tends to increase the audience's boredom.

Do not launch into production without being certain of having a complete portfolio of the ideas or events of the film. You might, perhaps, even start with the end of the film, to be certain of not missing it!

DOSE

So that a film should not degenerate into an imposition and become boring, it should be dosed with various elements. Sustaining the audience's interest is a problem which preoccupies the minds of all film directors.

One might possibly object that animated films run little risk of this, on the grounds that they are in the category of the mini-shorts.

I think it is a mistake to believe this, and I think that a three minute film could seem to be too long if it were not well balanced.

We must not forget, either, that animated films are more tiring on the eyes and demanding of attention from an audience than normal films, since animation is a concentration of ideas and images which require a certain effort on their part and consequently are liable to create tension.

It is rare for a spectator (with the exception of the afficionados) to grasp immediately on the first showing, all the ideas contained in an animated film. (I am, of course, speaking mostly of films with some kind of philosophical pretension).

LAUGHTER

If you make a film which is didactic in inspiration, you have to allow some moments of relaxation, and remember that laughter has a far more emphatic educational potential than a moralising atmosphere.

If the audience occasionally bursts into laughter at the most tragic moment in a particularly sombre film, it is because the creator has forgotten to allow them the essential moment of relaxation after a period of great tension.

POETRY

The poetry which is indispensable to any work of art may be born of the picture itself (naive drawings, limited animation) or of the ideas.

It is perhaps one of the most difficult things to define. The poetic atmosphere of a film is not put together, but distilled gradually by the writer's state of mind. Now, there are some writers who are not poets. Why do all of Trnka's films bear the imprint of this poetry which transfigures simple dolls, while many other animators of puppets, in spite of a perfect technique, are not able to give them a soul?

THE IRRATIONAL

This, again, is a purely personal point of view, but I think that the animation cinema is gaining more and more on the live action cinema in the sphere of surrealism and irrationality.

In this field, it has the advantage in that it can invent anything. Trick photography in the live action cinema remains limited, and the imagination is conditioned by these limits. In animation, on the other hand, it is the imagination which has to gallop after the artist's hand, for it can do practically anything. The writer is hardly able to take full advantage of it.

So it is becoming more and more obvious that the animation cinema can and must invent the future. It must become forward looking. That endeavour may be applied, in my opinion, in any production, whether a commercial, industrial or experimental film. The greatest difficulty is now, as it always has been, that of convincing the producer.

SATIRE

This, too, is indispensable in making the audience think. But on this point we can certainly not reproach animators who have, for years, been making liberal use of this element.

CHILDREN'S FILMS

Please allow me to put in brackets my comment on animated cartoons for children. I shall simply ask one question. Is it really necessary to conceive programmes as specially for children, considering that most children see animated films with so much more enthusiasm, receptivity, comprehension and poetic feeling than most people who are termed adults?

Each time I have presented animated films, even difficult ones, to an audience of children, I have noticed that they penetrate the films with no

Ernest and Giselle Ansorge
Storyboard from *Fantasmatic*
(pages 68–69)

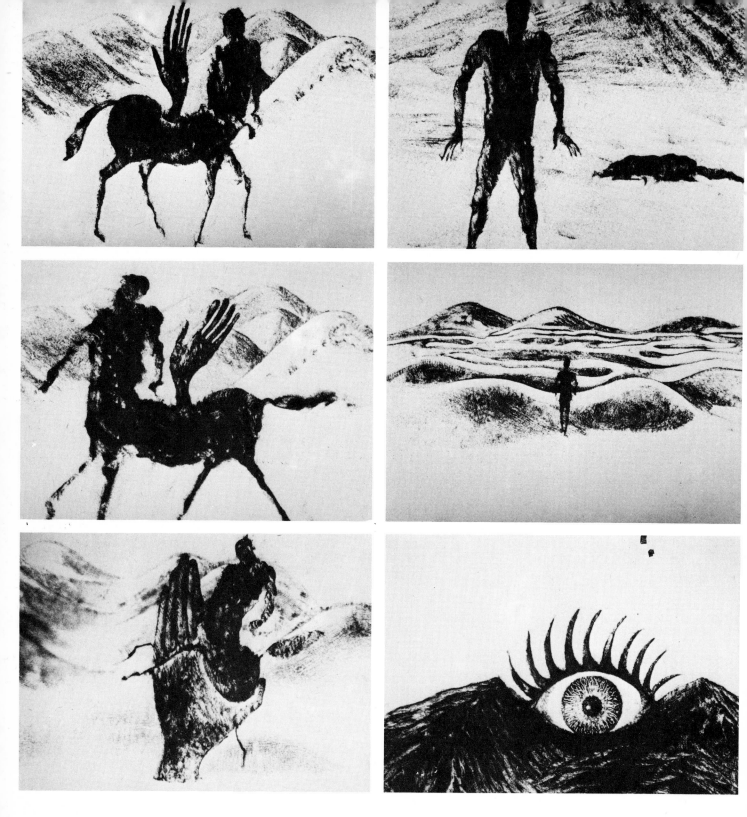

difficulty, that they catch most of the nuances and that they are often thoughtful and inflexible critics.

Irrationality, on the other hand, does not worry them. I would suggest rather a special information class for "difficult" adults who have a block against the animation cinema.

Children frequently reject animated films which are made for them, because they consider them to be "made for children",

As a conclusion to these few reflections based on my experience (experience of a small production team and with just a couple of animators) a script worked out by this modest team is inspired by the daily life of the team, and its tone would vary according to the circumstances and impressions of the moment.

In this respect, I think of the film *Moonbird* by the Hubleys, which seems to stem directly from this homely method. *Moonbird* is to me an exemplary film.

7. TYPOGRAPHY IN MOTION

Eino Ruutsalo (Finland)

It is not surprising that one visual medium should be the inspiration source for another. Eino Ruutsalo, the Finnish artist, used letter symbols as a starting point for expansion and ABC123 turned out to be a very humanistic film overlayed with some elements of emotion.

The possible expansion of some old visual signs of letters and numbers overlayed with the added dimension of motion and sound can work quite successfully, as is proved by Ruutsalo.

ABC 123

By chance I picked up two books illustrating typefaces, an old book and a new one. The old one contained various ornamentations, vignettes and old typefaces from illuminated initials to outlandish letters. This book created a sensation of pure handicraft. The new book was very systematic. It, too, had various sizes of type, marks and signs, but it gave the impression of having been made by a computer.

Those two books were two opposing worlds. The one romantic, peaceful and decorative. The other, hurried, chilly and void of feeling. The contrast between these two easily identifiable and emotionally charged feelings began to awaken my interest. In me, the impression began to generate a series of situations and I could not prevent myself from comparing the pages, placing the letters in various groups—after all, I had for a long time constructed pages out of typefaces with more written symbols. I had been making them with wooden founts discarded by the printer, or on a borrowed first-class electric typewriter with adjustable stroke pressure.

I had in front of me here the same values: softness and hardness, love and violence, human rights and the denial of them. The books had no intrinsic value, and my scissors had already begun to cut out the border decorations pages and flourishes. Or my pencil had begun to draw new shapes upon the typeset page. Those letters seemed to contain tales ready writ. One merely had to learn to read that extraordinary way of writing. The letters could not be taken to represent the sounds assigned to them and which, marshalled in a learned pattern, would produce an intelligible word. The personality of the letters had to be approached from other angles.

By their appearance alone, some of the letters were cheerful while others were ugly. Some were chubby and others ailing, proud or subdued, well-meaning or aggressive. A group formed out of a specific letter was relaxed, a group formed out of another was restless and loud. Three arbitrary letters put together formed a strange combination of imagined symbols, codes of secret plans, abbreviations of non-existing associations and concepts—the game seemed an infinite one.

It seemed as though every letter had a pre-designed meaning; a single letter was in a sense a whole word or concept. A single letter certainly meant different things to different people. By using some letters, a tragedy might be written. With others, a pure farce. With some letters, declarations of love might be made. And only some letters seemed suitable for writing a complaint to a government office.

I selected a number of letters and tried them out on myself—to find out what person might be brought to my mind by any letter. S—Sartre; L—Lennon; M—Monroe; R—Rousseau; T—Tarzan; I—Ionesco . . . I looked up their pictures somewhere—and an alphabet of a different kind was ready.

I noticed that the three first letters of the alphabet—A, B and C—like the first numerals 1, 2 and 3—were a sort of synthesis of a message that I wished to pass on. The message that I wish to have passed on from person to person was actualy the symbol of the ideals of any one of us—a theme that we tried to convey, to make heart, around which we wished to gather others who think alike.

I did not feel a need to define my ideal in concrete terms, but only to defend the opportunity of everybody to declare their own. I knew that there are always forces and counter-forces. The film became the procession, the demonstration, the revolt, the proclamation of the typeface.

The glued-up, drawn and combined compositions were photographed on high contrast film, to eliminate the marks of glue and the grey tones. Then a large positive copy was made on film. (The example shown includes several themes). By placing each frame on the clouded glass of the editing table, the characters could be filmed and then timed to produce the right length. As the occasion required, I made the film in black and white or in colour. I treated the black and white negative with colour here and there—as I often do—and then I got a final colour negative completed, to get a copy from. I recorded the monotonous sound of a printing press, working in ever repeating movements, to get a general sound through the whole. Now and then I broke off the background sound, and inserted sound that expressed the sentiment of the type characters.

In order to see how mighty is the message of letters, we rise towards the end of this short film above the procession of letters and, as if from an aeroplane gliding past, we see the rows of letters and numerals extending all the way to the horizon, the masses of ever-new ideals.

Eino Ruutsalo (next page)
The novelty about Ruutsalo's *ABC 123* is its clever use of typography translated onto the screen and the organic changes to human characters from letters and figures.

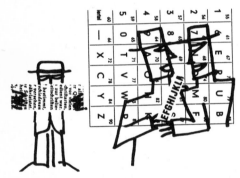

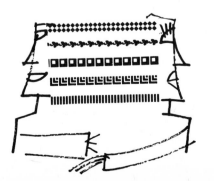

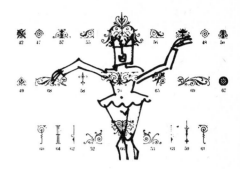

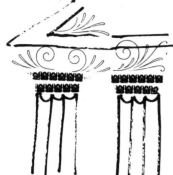

4 cicero

СЛѢДС
СЛѢД

Слѣдствіемъ введенія въ Россіи книгопечатанія
было введеніе типографщики... пріобрѣ-
тающее ... и болѣе важнѣйшихъ, не смо-
тря ... сконное упрямство ... повержен-
цовъ ... и древнихъ рукописей ... священно
и независимо начали ... мъ ... книж-
... ковъ, которыхъ ... списыва-
... книгъ. Типографское дѣло, вопреки мнѣ-
СЛѢДСТВIЕМЪ ВВЕДЕНIЯ ВЪ РОССIИ К
№ 1234567890

2 Cicero

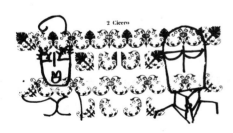

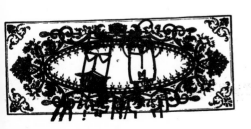

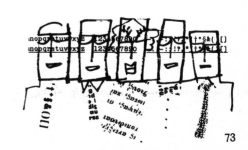

8. SCRIPTWRITING FOR ANIMATION

Joy Batchelor (G.B.)

Joy Batchelor has written many hundreds of scripts for both live action and animated films She is able to combine literary with visual talents, a rare gift in visual communication. Possibly her best known work is the film adaptation of George Orwell's *Animal Farm* together with Philip Stapp and John Halas. She has also adapted and directed Gilbert and Sullivan's *Ruddigore* and several sponsored films for BP, Shell and the World Health Organisation for whom she is presently acting as consultant.

Film is a means of communication through the use of moving pictures, words and sound, with the added dimension of time. It employs visuals, music, sound, story and words in a varying tempo and within a given time to achieve its effect. Animated film is based on ideas, graphic design, fantasy and physical impossibilities—not on realism, which is the main basis for live action film and television.

Animation is a small part of the mass media group which includes film, television, the press and radio, all of which must communicate with a large audience. All are subject to the economic background of the country of origin and none of them can exist without a paying audience —and a large one at that.

Production costs in all mass media are substantial. Animation is no exception and if an audience does not like the product it does not buy it. Newspapers, magazines and cinemas have been closing down for years. Only television can afford to send the audiences to sleep because they happen to be at home in an easy chair.

It follows that a scriptwriter must possess or acquire the ability to attract and sustain the interest of any given audience and communicate in terms of the medium for the length of the animated film, whether it be fifteen seconds or ninety minutes. Animation is a group activity and a scriptwriter must learn the 'language' of animation in order to think in terms of it and be able to work as one of the team of producer, director, animators, designers, camera and sound men.

ANIMATION IDEAS

Animation may be said to start with an idea and although ideas are not the sole province of the scriptwriter, his is the main responsibility for providing the content and structure of the film in a workable form and within the budget. Although the budget is the responsibility of the producer, the scriptwriter has to be aware of it to avoid the common pitfall of gaily writing in crowd scenes or battles on land or sea, etc. which are costly and unrewarding to animate, and better left to live action. The great strength of animation lies in its power to make literal that which is normally figurative, in its power of exaggeration in order to present ideas with impact, its ability to project a

thought until it obtains an entirely new and more truthful aspect. Add to this the world of fantasy inherent in animation and you have the factors which enable the smallest and poorest member of the mass media, animated film, to make its own contribution to human experience.

The potential subject matter is challenging and the production can range from seven second television commercials to the four to fifteen minute sponsored films for education, information propaganda or goodwill, right up to the feature length 70–90 minute entertainment film. Perhaps the most usual format is the 7-minute short cartoon, made famous by Walt Disney and continued by Hanna-Barbera and many others. These films used to be shown in the cinema—today they are seen on the 'box'. They are sometimes strung together to make a 25 minute programme and sometimes extended to a 60 minute special.

All on its own is the film beloved by every animator—the one he makes for himself. Depending on the idea, luck, talent, good timing and judgement, the film-maker's faith in his own idea may bring him a large audience and some money, or an audience of one and a total loss of the cost of making the film.

In every one of these categories, both content and audience can vary considerably.

In America, where the cost of production can be recovered from a vast home market on sponsored television time, the majority of short animated films are made to amuse family audiences. By now the form has become a stereotype. The hero has adventures, thrills, a battle or a chase, and finally overcomes the villain, usually against all odds. The use of gags throughout the film supplies the humour—these films *must* be funny. The tempo is fast, the sound loud, the effects increasingly take the place of animation. The timing and continuity are impeccable, but the content leaves much to be desired and altogether too much violence is used to achieve crude laughs. There are reassuring signs that this long tradition is being eroded, but it is a slow process, considering that we receive on British television the programmes seen on American television the year before!

In England the economic pattern is different again, and the type of film has been determined by it. Very few British animated films were ever shown in the cinemas because it was cheaper to buy existing American films. This applies to British television today.

SPONSORED AND DOCUMENTARY CARTOONS

What evolved in England was the sponsored film; first, Government sponsorship during World War II and for some years after, under the Labour Government, and since then by large industrial companies. The subjects varied—so did the audience. The subject may be hydraulics, the audience a specialised group of technical people. It may be how a computer works in terms that can be understood by a lay audience, or the working of an oil refinery or whisky distillery to a lay audience for goodwill purposes—improving the Company 'image'.

IDEA INTO SCRIPT

It is important to know at the outset what kind of effect the film is intended to produce on the audience. Is it to teach or to inform? It may be the trickiest problem of all, to explain the necessity of something like National Insurance in Britain, or damming the Delta in Holland, and to explain it briefly, clearly and with humour, so that when the film audience in due course becomes the taxpayer for such schemes, he will do so, hopefully, with a better grace.

A sponsored film is based on the briefing since the structure of the script (and the film) depends on it. When the briefing is incomplete, it is up to the scriptwriter to prise the information out of the sponsor. In a sense the sponsor is also the audience, since he will be paying for the production.

Given the subject of the film and its objective, plus a well defined policy on the approach to the particular audience, the next step is research into the subject. This should be extensive, for it is during this stage that the subconscious takes over from time to time. This is the point when the ideas formulate, leading to the creation of characters and story and situation, all based on the briefing but transformed into something of interest, instead of a categorical summing up of information, a logical retailing of facts. Film scripting has its own logic, but it differs vastly from the form of a pamphlet.

E. M. Forster compares this creative dip into the subconscious to lowering a bucket into a well. There are times when any scriptwriter can cry "There's a hole in my bucket!", but at such times a deadline works wonders. The essential story, as it emerges from the collected facts, must proceed from the medium. Situations must arise from the story and they must be visual at idea stage. It is a stern discipline, but the economy of means is part of the strength of animation in putting ideas across.

As a case in point I quote from an article written on the scripting of a film made back in 1947: *Charley's March of Time*", made by Halas & Batchelor Cartoon Films Ltd.

"This film, one of a series, was sponsored by the C.O.I.: the brief to inform the public of the working of the National Insurance Act due to operate from July 1948. In addition to giving factual information on payments and benefits, the film had an additional 'goodwill' job to perform.

"General knowledge on this subject can only be fragmentary. We had to gather up these pieces of knowledge and transform them into a unified statement in terms of movement, design and time.

Making the general public feel pleased to pay up to 6/2d (quite a sum then) a week for insurance did not sound promising. Nor did the benefits—sickness, unemployment, widow's benefit, death grant—present anything but morbid visual associations. Research into the subject provided a mountain of historical facts in addition to the original briefing on the Act itself. But it was not until we remembered that our medium can play tricks with time, that our two main script problems were resolved.

"Our central character, Charley, might carp at paying out good money now to insure against a host of unpleasant future possibilities. But in any former existence he would have been glad to get off so cheaply.

"The main structure of the film becomes established. Facts first. Benefits and payments are explained officially by a commentator to the central character, and the public is informed at the same time. Charley reacts in much the same way as the public does—he objects. When a cartoon character objects he can go a lot further than the public. When Charley says indignantly: 'I'd rather go back to the days before we had any of your wonderful insurance!' he can—and does —go back to the earliest form of life on earth.

"With Charley arbitrarily placed by the medium of the cartoon in a position where he can experience his age-old struggles for security, both he and the audience can, in the process, learn to value comprehensive insurance instead of scorning it.

"Situations arose from this story naturally enough. Embryo Charley was forced to discover the security of dry land to avoid being eaten by bigger creatures. The first man to discover a cave—again Charley—was looking for security— this time from dinosaur. Mediaeval Charley was obliged to build a castle in order to be safe from marauding bands. Nor did his trouble end there. In succeeding centuries he was exposed to unemployment, sickness, industrial injury and the penury of old age. With considerable relief he returns to the social security of 1948".

This film was made a long time ago—the situation was different. The audience and the mood was completely different. The very people who look at films are different—they are all more than twenty years older, and some of course had yet to be born. The generation that has grown up with televison is more sophisticated visually, its thinking and approach to life, its values and ethics are all changed, some for the better, some for the worse. The pace has quickened. The approach and tone are different.

The latest sponsored film to come my way was called *The Five*. It was intended to teach footcare to girls of 11 + years. Quite obviously the didactic approach was out. So was the voice of Authority. The appeal to this particular audience *had* to be emotional and it is well nigh impossible to be emotional about a foot. There were other considerations to take into account. Young girls today buy shoes for fashion. This was intended as a long-life film, and as shoe shapes change yearly, actually showing shoes was out. Showing deformed feet was out for no young girl of 12 can be expected to identify herself with what she will become twenty or thirty years later, as a direct result of badly fitting shoes.

After a number of false starts, the basic idea of using five toes as the five main characters, was put forward. Five toes, with the capacity to change into five sisters complaining at the end of a hard day's footwork, of the bad treatment their careless owner had meted out to them and dreaming of a world in which they could grow up straight and strong.

The difference in thinking and approach over a span of twenty years is considerable in this small area. During this time the format of the sponsored animated films was to influence a number of short entertainment films, one of them, *Automania 2000* being of particular interest to me.

STORYBOARD OF SCENE BREAKDOWN

Normally the director takes over from the scriptwriter when the storyboard is approved, and takes responsibility for timing, scene breakdown and overall control of animation. The number of drawings grows so that the production storyboard consists of shot by shot pictures with camera movements and character action indicated on each one. A scene breakdown chart is prepared corresponding with the production storyboard. The chart is a visual control record of the number of scenes and the production stage reached at any point, plus the people employed in various departments and basic data, like deadlines. It is customary to record and chart the music before the animation stage is reached so that animators can work to precise timing and because it is too costly to animate 'wild' footage. It is usual to record a guide commentary or voice track as soon as the timing is completed. During this time the scriptwriter will only be called in, like the doctor, when something has gone wrong. When the cutting copy of the film is assembled, he may be needed again to cut the talk, where the picture has taken over, or to write in new lines because the picture is not making the necessary point.

Automania 2000 broke many of these rules and broke them successfully. The script began as an idea suggested in a scientific article: a new idea at that time (1963), but very much part of current thinking today. Briefly, it set forth the proposition that technology would take over and that man would be exterminated by his own ingenuity. Instead of preparing a full script prior to production, this film evolved in a series of talking sessions, based on a skeleton framework. The enormous advantage of this apparent lack of method was that

the film was kept fluid throughout production and a number of subsidiary ideas were incorporated during the making of it. This was a fortunate production in the sense that those in the group of people involved were all able to contribute right the way along, and the film is as valid today—and as powerful, as when it was made.

The commentary was constantly revised and this, though difficult, meant that it could be improved and help the picture. Now that this particular theme of technological pollution is common knowledge, many of the words need not be spoken, but the place of words in an animated film has always been a moot point.

Ideally, animation could and should be able to be shown all over the world without any words at all. But in hard fact, animation now relies heavily on words, in sponsored and in commercial entertainment fields, because it is cheaper to write amusing dialogue than it is to animate a comic situation.

It follows, that to write successfully in these fields the scriptwriter must belong to the country of origin of the film, or must at any rate, live there for the duration.

This is tough on British scriptwriters in animation since there is not a great enough home market, either in the cinemas or television, to pay the costs of production in features or shorts— apart from lucky breaks.

FULL LENGTH TV PRODUCTION

There has been, nevertheless, a solitary occasion to script a one-hour television special. It was based on the Gilbert and Sullivan comic opera *Ruddigore*, one of their lesser known works, lasting for over two hours on stage.

The most obvious step was to edit it to size, and the next to decide what to keep, what to discard, what to change in the way of action and locale since one of the conditions of making the film was that no words or songs be altered or rewritten.

A take-off of a 19th century melodrama, the story concerns a luckless baronet who has inherited the witch's curse laid on his family in reprisal for being burnt. This story, complicated by many subplots, and changes of identity of most of the main characters, was asking a lot of an essentially simple medium. A cartoon character, to succeed, has to remain in character. In addition, much of the story was sung, which made it that much more difficult to grasp. On stage, a song has repeats and encores. On film, and even more in television, there is only the present moment to get the point across. Fully half of the film had, necessarily, to be devoted to establishing characters and situations—far too long. The second half provided the valid justification for animation. The supernatural took over. Fantasy, in the form of ghosts coming to the rescue of the hero to provide the predictable happy ending, was an overdue relief, for most of the action could well have been live.

Transposing this two hour long comic opera into a one hour animated television special required great industry—breakdown into sixteen sequences, some had as many as 72 scenes. It also required much talent in "character animation", a little known art today.

This was intended as a "cultural film". The main trouble was that it was not the culture of the day and Gilbert & Sullivan were not in any position to update the words and music to make it acceptable to a different age and audience. For all that, as a cultural film, it has a devoted if small audience and for some reason I will never fathom, it went down best in Pittsburg!!

FEATURE ANIMATION

Ruddigore is the only British production to date of an animated TV special. The situation in films for the cinema is only slightly better. Two feature length animated films have been made in Britain, both with American backing, both with American advisers, both aimed at an Anglo-American audience—*Animal Farm* based on the book by George Orwell, Produced and Directed by John Halas and Joy Batchelor, made during 1952–54; and *Yellow Submarine* made by George Dunning of TV Cartoons, in 1967.

Both won critical acclaim, but neither won the world wide audience that only Disney has managed to achieve in the cinema.

A feature length animated film has to sustain interest over a long time and it is a much more condensed and compelling form of film than live action. This exacting quality can tire an audience, especially one brought up on the undemanding daily fare of television.

The audacious shock tactics and eclectic visuals of *Yellow Submarine*, while delighting many, demanded altogether too much of an average audience, particularly when the strength of the graphics and sound was not supported by a strong story. This, to my mind, is the first requirement of a feature length film. It must be a strong story that cannot be told in live action. This rare quality may be the reason why *Animal Farm* has enjoyed such a long life as a film, and why more people have seen it years after it was made than when it originally came out.

I am profoundly indebted to Dr. Roger Manvell for his permission to draw freely from his documentation of the scripting of *Animal Farm.*

ANIMAL FARM

By George Orwell, is a book with a very strong idea. It is a fable about aninals, but these animals are as serious on their attitude to life as any cow or pig or dog or fowl you may meet on a real farm. They are not sentimentalised to suit human prejudices, nor are they cutely humanised like most animals in cartoon films. For George Orwell's fable is symbolic, like Swift's story in which Lemuel Gulliver travels to the land of the Horses, and the result is a political satire full of deep feeling. The animals on a badly run farm revolt against its cruel and drunken owner, drive him out by means of an organised revolution, and set up their own form of democratic community, led by the pigs, who prove to be the most intelligent of the animals. But although they begin with a democracy, it gradually develops into a dictatorship in which the pigs are the herrenvolk, and Napoleon, the most powerful and evil of the pigs, is the dictator. In the book, the final stage is the saddest, for the pigs wear clothes and banquet with the enemies of animal-kind, the cunning and cruel human exploiters of their wealth and labour. In the film, a happier twist is given to this situation by showing that the animals are yet again capable of organising resistance against the leaders who have betrayed them.

"To turn this satire into an animated film was to face the issue of dramatising an animal story in which the characters must be as seriously portrayed as in a human story. No animal could be sentimentalised for the sake of box-office—the idea behind the story would not permit this. Once the story was selected, a new kind of cartoon film was to be made—a serious cartoon. A style of presentation in sound and image must be evolved to interpret this on the screen, and the essential incidents in the book planned out in dramatic shape and continuity. To effect this analysis, a breakdown chart was prepared, showing all the characters in their various relationships to the plot and to each other. It was obvious that certain animal and human characters, in which the book is naturally prolific (like Mollie, the vain and parasitic white pony), would have to recede into the background or be eliminated altogether, so that those animals and humans most concerned with developing the action and characterising the clash of interests could be kept in the foreground.

TENSION CHART

"A tension chart was prepared on a long stretch of paper folding into sections like a map. The story line (the development of action and situation) was worked out along the top. Immediately underneath, a tension line showed how the dramatic expectancy should operate for the audience as the action progressed—working up to a climax, relaxing afterwards, then gathering tension for the next phase of excitement, throughout the total length of the film. This ensured that there should be no excessive lulls in the action—that the quiet, cumulative excitement and concentration generated by reading a book to oneself could be translated into the extrovert clash of the drama, the rise and fall of action capable of holding the attention

Main Story	Jones goes to bed.	Animals awake and go into barn.	Old Major makes speech on revolution to come.	Animals enthusiastic. Sing Revolutionary hymn so loud that....	...they wake Jones who fires his gun.	Animals disappear into stables.
Tension						
Mood	Expectant	– Excited	– Enthusiastic		Climax	
Music	Subdued	Inspiring	Song works to climax		Silence	Subdued
Colour	Moonlight	Exterior colours			Dark	
Time of day	Night between 10 p.m. and Midnight					
Time of year	Midsummer					

Part of the 'tension chart' specially devised for the production to plot the high points and the mood for the production of *Animal Farm*.

Jones returns with farm hands.	Snowball despatches the animals.	Fight.	Jones and men make for the gateway.	Jessy is dead	Animals destroy relics of slavery and run up flag.
Expectation		Anger and excitement		Sorrow	Jubilati
Gradual ..... build		Dynamic		Quiet	Inspiring
Normal		effects		Cold	Normal
					Through
					Midsummer

Animals unfed. Animals get hungrier.	Jones sleeps drunkenly. Animals get restive.	Hungry animals raid food store.	Jones wakes.	Animals turn and chase Jones away from farm.	

Progressive repression and	Discontent	Revolt	Suppression	Open revolt	
building up to			Crash effect	Fight between animals & Jones (staccato)	
light getting harsher				Hard clear colours	
Through day			Through day		
			Midsummer		

Sunday
ways

urch

volutionary ng.	Enter farm building.	They inspect the house.	Napoleon steals the puppies.	Animals leave house. Pledge not to enter again.	Snowball paints out Manor Farm and paints in Animal Farm.

	Distrust and Suspicion	Distrust	Aggression	Determination	Jubilation
ng	Subdued	Subdued	Sinister note	Determined	Jubilation
ight		Dark interior		Clear	Optimistic
			Day		
					July

Within the barn what goes
on can only be guessed.

Shortly after, inside the
barn the hens are revealed
at the base of the platform.
They are huddled together
tied and guarded by two dogs.
Napoleon, surrounded by dogs,
Squealer at his side, rises
to make a speech.

The rest of the animals,
who have been specially
assembled, crouch together
in apprehension.

of an assembled audience for all of 75 minutes. Immediately beneath the tension line were comments to guide the visual and aural realisation of the action—the mood of the scene (expectant, sorrowful, aggressive, jubilant, angry, climactic). Under this were comments to guide the composer, for music comes very early into the process of animation since drawn movements depend to a greater rather than a lesser extent on the rhythm of the musical score prepared in advance. Next in the tension chart came guidance for the dominant colour-theme (moonlight, darkness, daylight, normal colour, cold colour, bright colour, or, with an indication of mood, in hard colour, 'getting harsher', or even 'optimistic'). Last came the time and season lines, indicating period of day or night and the season of the year.

"When this chart had been discussed, criticised and modified until the shape, feeling, colour and mood of the story seemed satisfactory in dramatic terms, a script was prepared in the form of a first treatment. By now the characters were taking on a preliminary shape in the minds of the directors, and the first drawings were lying about all over the place, at home and in the studio. Some of the drawings were accompanied by brief verbal descriptions (like this for the pig called Major: 'Old and dignified. Ponderous. Always seen lying down, drawing must suggest his size and weight within limited movement allowed'), and notes were made on the relationship of the characters to each other, like the devoted companionship of Boxer the great cart-horse, and Benjamin the donkey, so that they could be designed both as an ensemble and as individual characters.

STORYBOARD

So far the work had been carried out by John Halas and myself. For the next stage a colleague, Philip Stapp, was called in to help prepare the storyboard, consisting of some 350 drawings and accompanying text, a kind of massive strip-cartoon of the future production. The satisfactory completion of this stage marked the end of the preparatory work, which had been confined conveniently to two or three individuals. Other artists were now brought in, and a graded form of team-work really began with the scene breakdown, on which, in the case of *Animal Farm* four artists were briefed to work, in addition to John Halas and myself. So far the period of preparation had taken some sixteen weeks.

"The scene breakdown is a series of hundreds of rough drawings indicating the breakdown of the film into a shot-by-shot treatment. These pictures are small (about 6 × 8 in) and quickly replaceable, reflecting the present fluid state in the detailed conception of how the film will move from shot to shot. It is here that the animated film differs widely in technique, though not in result, from the live-action film. Certain designers of live-action films make considerable use of small drawings to guide the nature of their future camera set-ups. The opening sequence of *Oliver Twist*, for example, was prepared on the drawing board by the designer John Bryan. Alfred Hitchcock's scripts are normally illustrated with shot-by-shot sketches, and Walt Disney has carried the storyboard technique over from his animated to his live-action productions, to assist his designers, directors and editors.

"But the fundamental difference remains—in a live-action film a sketch is a blueprint for translation through a three-dimensional set and real-life action, back into a two-dimensional photograph, which is not in itself at all the same thing as the guiding initial sketch. In an animated film the actual shot to be seen by the audience is created directly on the drawing-board, and the sketch on the storyboard is the germ for the finished drawing which is to follow. Both the shot itself and the editing process (the montage of the film) are entirely created on paper, the camera merely being used as a recording device, and not as a creative, photographic art assisting in the interpretation and feeling of the film, as the camera does when it is sensitively used in live-action work. The storyboard is therefore the real beginning of the production process—the shaping of the shots, the evolution of the montage. The storyboard for *Animal Farm* filled the walls of two rooms. On the floor were baskets full of discarded drawings.

SHOOTING SCRIPT

"Parallel with the growth of the storyboard, the shooting script was being prepared. Writing and drawing for the film emerged together from the endless discussion which is natural at this crucial stage in the work. The drama developed now into the sequences foreseen as early as the stage of the tension chart; action and situation were now being clarified. Six weeks' work resolved itself into a film of eighteen sequences—planned in the form of the storyboard sketches and the typed script. At the same time, the characterisation of the chief animals reached a degree of finality, so that their appearance, nature and behaviour could be defined for each stage of the action. When action and characters had been approved by all concerned, the first stages of actual animation (and the detailed studies and researches which go with it) could begin, in close association with the narration, dialogue, sound effects and music written or indicated in the script.

NARRATION AND DIALOGUE

Dialogue and narration in an animated film present different technical problems. Audiences do not on the whole respond to the kind of narration which stands between them and their direct experience of the film. It is irritating to be told

John Halas and Joy Batchelor
The initial storyboard version for Britain's first full length film *Animal Farm* based on George Orwell's classic novel. Several other visual storyboards in pencil as well as in colour followed before the film was ready for production (opposite).

something in words when you want to be left alone to observe it directly for yourself. On the other hand, narration can in a few explanatory words cover elements of a story which would not dramatise well, or which would upset the dramatic balance of the film if presented directly in all their detail. In the script for *Animal Farm*, the narration was kept to a few unobtrusive sentences, and these in turn were not dubbed into the film until it was complete, so that phrases and sentences could be added or deleted according to the final needs of the drama. Dialogue, on the other hand, was needed throughout the film, both for humans and animals, and since the animation depended on every mouth-movement of the words, the dialogue had to be made final before the animation itself began. The dialogue used was entirely that of George Orwell's book, which is direct and simple and confined to essentials. The natural sounds, on the other hand, were all used to increase the effects of realism—the sounds used were mostly the real sounds of a farm, the cries of animals, the creaking of wheels and machinery, the sounds in fact, which would be made by the natural counterparts to the objects in the drawn images on the screen.

MUSICAL ELEMENT

"In most live-action films (other than musicals) the composition of the musical scene follows the completion of shooting and the rough-cut stage of editing. The composer then meets the director, views the film accompanied by its dialogue and effects tracks, and works out with him those sections of the action which require the emotional support and emphasis which music can so potently add to the production. The music, which is the last creative contribution to most live-action films is one of the first in the case of the animated film.

"Since the animation should, in many scenes in the film, closely reflect the rhythms of the music, the score must be composed before the full process of animation starts. To show how the animation must respond to every phase of musical developments, a music chart is prepared as a guide to the animator. This chart relates picture to sound frame by frame. The composer's work therefore is one of great responsibility, more especially in a cartoon with a serious theme, like *Animal Farm*. Technical dexterity and ingenuity in scoring to

Animal Farm.
Artwork from the finished production.

show off the equivalent complexity of the animation is not enough. *Animal Farm* as a book has many exceptional qualities. It is a fable about animals who are not mere storybook creatures; their life on the farm is presented by an author who was familiar with both farm life and animal life. There is, in his writing, not only a lyrical feeling for the countryside, but also a down-to-earth realism; the animals are quite uncompromising in their behaviour, which is often savage and cruel and dirty as well as loyal and devoted. There is satire and tragedy and melodrama in the book. The music can do much to enable the audience to respond to the emotions of the animals as they pass through their bitter experience in exchanging one cruel yoke for another of their own making. They must hope and suffer, they must sing and weep, and they must learn by hard experience what happens when they are too optimistic, simple-minded and trusting. The composer must understand this at script-stage and make music for the animals which reflects, for our better understanding, their striving and their passion. For George Orwell's harshness as a writer was the direct result of his own deep human feeling. The work of composing the music for this film was carried out by Matyas Seiber, who had previously prepared scores for many of the short animated films made by the Halas & Batchelor unit before he undertook the music for *Animal Farm.*

"Matyas Seiber's music does not at every stage attempt to follow the details of action point by point. This would be to reduce the status of the music throughout the film to that of providing sound effects. The interpretation and emphasis of mood remain at certain stages the chief purpose of the score for *Animal Farm*, and this is done by allowing the music to develop its own unique qualities in the expression of emotion. It serves to bind together the various sequences and add to the sense of continuity of the film. Many of the individual sections of the score form long compositions of some minutes' duration. But at other stages in the film the composer must be prepared to subordinate completely the nature of his work to the details of the action, and permit it to become a colourful elaboration of sound effect. The composer must work in the closest association with the film-makers, or his work, however, beautiful or atmospheric in itself, will tend to draw away from the immediate needs of the film. The orches-tration of the score for *Animal Farm* was designed for performance by thirty-six instruments."

In quoting so freely I am reminded that it is only too easy to forget the thinking over three years recalled twenty years later and a work diary is invaluable·

POINTERS FOR SCRIPTWRITERS

Perhaps the most difficult aspect of such an exacting task is to maintain the liveliness of the idea throughout the long and laborious processes needed to bring it to the screen in the form of film. As Louis de Rochemont, our American associate on this film, once said: "Nobody ever tried to make a bad film." This certainly applies to scriptwriters and I can only hope that these guidelines may help those scriptwriters, with the talent and devotion needed for the task, to write good scripts which can become good films.

The rules for the scriptwriter remain valid; he *must* communicate with today's audience in terms it can appreciate. The storyboard stage is the best time to try to evaluate audience reaction. For the first time the film-to-be has ceased to be a string of ideas in somebody's mind or words on paper and has evolved into a series of pictures in continuity, with sound and action typed alongside the pictures.

The number of pictures will vary with the length and content of the film; for a five minute film sixty storyboard pictures are normal. The more reactions there are from people to the story-board at this stage, the better. Weaknesses in structure and irrelevant ideas can be spotted and during the group discussion over the storyboard better solutions can be found. This, while trying to the scriptwriter, usually contributes to a better end-result.

The picture side of the storyboard is of value to the scriptwriter whether he can draw or not, since it forces him to think in visual terms as well as verbal. At the same time the overall progression of the storyboard can be studied and, if necessary, re-shaped. This, again, can demoralise the writer, until he gains the experience to understand that, while changes hurt, it is as well to avoid three climaxes (and anti-climaxes) at script stage *before* production starts, rather than when the film is finished.

9. WRITING DIALOGUE FOR ANIMATION

Roger Macdougall (G.B.)

Professor Roger MacDougall enjoyed a reputation as a playwright in England as well as a scriptwriter working for the Ealing Studios. He was responsible for the scripts of *The Man in the White Suit* and *The Mouse that Roared*, both outstanding film comedies. His experience as an animated film writer arose when working with Halas and Batchelor and the Larkins studios in London. His skill lies in his ability to write words on three levels. His lines immediately inspire visual images. They have compact literary meaning always to the point of the argument which is advanced and illuminated by its content. They are also set in an easy stanza form—both enjoyable to read and compose music for.

Roger MacDougall became the first professor in scriptwriting when he accepted an appointment as Head of Scriptwriting at the Theatre Arts Faculty —University of California at Los Angeles.

When I first tackled animation, many years ago, I made no attempt to contribute towards the visual part of the film by anything so practical as a suggestion or an idea. I confined myself to writing language which was visually evocative.

The first was a PR film with a running time of perhaps twenty minutes for the Imperial Chemical Industries, on the subject (later used as the title) of *Enterprise*. I began by writing commentary in a very free form of doggerel verse:

Consider the Ancient Potter
And the Ancient Potter's daughter.
They work with a will
Not only with energy, but with skill,
To make lots
Of pots.
Not only for themselves
Also they fill the shelves
Of their neighbours
With the fruits of their labours
An endless row—
Pot after pot
How do they know
They will all be bought?
Oh-oh
They're not!
This calls for thought,
Fierce heart-burning
Must the potter's wheel stop turning?
Is he redundant
Now that the pots are abundant?
Or can he master
Disaster?—   and so on.

I hope the reader sees from this what I mean by evocative writing. And I imagine he can see in his mind's eye a fairly accurate picture of the animation which eventually accompanied the words.

Even apparently recalcitrant subjects can be tackled by a writer in this way. I was asked to do one about ICI's balance sheet—an apparently formidable assignment. Here is how I started.

"Friends,
To make ends
Meet
Squarely in the middle
Without any fiddle
Some man replete
With talents
Invented the balance"

And on the subject of danger posed to the British chemical industry, by large combines growing up on the continent, this:

"These huge giants
Will pinch our clients
Send out the Clarion Call—
Divided, we fall.
United, on the other hand
We stand"

To my mind a writer can best contribute to an animated film by this kind of stimulating writing.

If he happens to have a visual imagination too, all to the good. But his visual imagination is unlikely to be as strong as that of someone trained in graphic art.

My contention is that a writer does not require a strongly developed visual sense in order to be able to contribute meaningfully to an animated film.

I am dealing here with animation in which commentary or dialogue is involved. I suppose a purist would claim that to resort to words in animation is an admission of defeat.

Though I appreciate the achievements of mime, like Marcel Marceau, and analogously the effect of an animated film which uses no words, I cannot agree that the effect of either technique would necessarily be ruined by the addition of words as well as sound (which is already used).

The words would have to be used sparingly and in a complementary way. But I believe with unrepentant obduracy that the added dimension of language *could* produce animated films of a higher order.

I can hear the storm of protest. Chaplin was ruined with the advent of talkies. But that was because Chaplin had perfected the art of silent film comedy, and the 'talkies' he produced were made in the infancy of that new medium. The result was a number of execrable scripts, redeemed only by the shining brilliance of his silent mime. He never became attuned to the new form. W. C. Fields and the Marx Brothers did, and their films, while still primitive, showed that the two elements of mime and dialogue could complement each other.

That is exactly what I feel about the cartoon. By refusing to explore the possibilities inherent in the addition of sync dialogue it is cutting itself off from possible expansion. I have a feeling that animation could best be served, not by orthodox speech, but by some form of zany Jabberwocky.

Visual from the film *Enterprise* by Peter Sacks (opposite).

My own early experience in the use of doggerel combined with cartoon makes me feel that the answer may well lie there. Sync doggerel in combination with cartoon characters is a possibility I would dearly like to explore.

Already the need to use distorted voices has been found to be essential. I would like to add the subtle distortion of the actual speech form which doggerel supplies, and perhaps go even further and distort the grammar and the syntax.

OBJECTIVES AND METHODS

Any writer, whatever his medium, uses language to paint in the mind of the reader or listener, or even spectator, a visual picture. Even abstract concepts are usually accompanied by some vague attempt at visualisation. In the case of a visual medium others are helping him to achieve his end. In a way this makes his problem more difficult, because he has to decide which parts of the picture can best be drawn by visuals alone, and which need language as well (I have already made my feelings about this clear).

The simplest example of language used alone is the printed word in a novel, or other form of book or article.

A radio play or documentary programme, adds to the simple use of words, the inflections of voices and the possibility of sound effects and music. A play in the theatre adds actors and lighting, costume and props.

A live action film adds much more. It is not limited in location, like a stage play. It can roam as freely as a novel or a radio play and yet adds all these other qualities I have described above.

Animation is the freest of all. It can add distortion, the achievement of the impossible, in fact, anything which the mind can conceive. This, one might think, would make animation the most effective of all the media. But I do not think even its most ardent supporter would claim that this is true.

It might be helpful to try to analyse why this should be so. Is it because a drawn character cannot have as much impact as a living person? This can hardly be true. Stand in front of the Mona Lisa—you can stand for half an hour lost in admiration. If the model from whom Leonardo da Vinci painted were available, I cannot see anyone standing before her for half an hour lost in speechless adoration. Leonardo did not just hold the mirror up to nature. He turned a piece of nature into a breathtaking experience.

And that must be the aim of the would-be artist in any medium, and the achievement of those who succeed, in communicating to the viewer, listener or reader a mind-expanding, timeless moment of awareness of something which surpasses the materials which make it up. This I hold to be true of all art.

Is live action film, then, the medium which can potentially achieve the greatest heights, since it next to animation, has most resources at its command, and also deals in a seeming reality?

Again, I feel the answer is no, perhaps because of these unlimited possibilities. A masterpiece in painting is limited and shaped, and has its content determined, by its frame. From moment to moment it is true, live action film is bounded by a frame also. But when the dimension of time is added the frame becomes almost meaningless. A film can go wherever it pleases. It has few limitations and is thus not forced into any discipline. For the creator it becomes difficult to choose, because the choice is so unlimited.

Another difficulty is the fact that live action film is essentially a group activity. This is not insuperable. Some of the masterpieces in architecture, particularly the early cathedrals, were achieved by many hands, as were many of the paintings in the great period of Italian painting.

But film to me still shows too much that need not be seen, too much that adds nothing to the effect. It is not sufficiently eclectic to be truly artistic. Others may disagree, but that is my feeling.

Unlike a good novelist, the film maker cannot prevent a great quantity of distracting material from intruding into his film.

It may be argued that this is like the descriptive material an author adds to give colour to his novel. But, of necessity, what is added to a film is not under the direct control of the creator. It is, partly at least, accidental. And I am not one of those who believe that uncontrolled accidents, like the pouring of paint on to canvas in a haphazard manner can produce anything worthy of the name of art.

A film is not, in the last analysis, a strip of celluloid, any more than a novel is a number of pages bound together between two cardboard covers, or a painting a piece of canvas daubed with colour. They are all in fact more rewardingly considered as experiences conveyed by the creator to the recipient, through different media.

The creator should always bear this in mind. He is creating an experience to be enjoyed. What he is doing is to make something happen in the mind of his audience.

If he is writing a film, nothing he writes has any intrinsic value of its own. It is to be judged solely by its effect on the viewer or the potential viewer.

If he is making a film, the less he shows on the screen that distracts the viewer and prevents him from concentrating on the essentials, the more successful the film will be.

What do all these observations add up to from the point of view of a writer about to tackle a script for an animated film?

Firstly, if it is a sponsored film for a client, then you are very likely to have some pretty dull material to put across. But do not despair. Try to find an approach, however oblique, which will tell your

Peter Sacks
Storyboard from the film *Enterprise*
designed and directed by Peter
Sacks for I.C.I. of Gt. Britain.

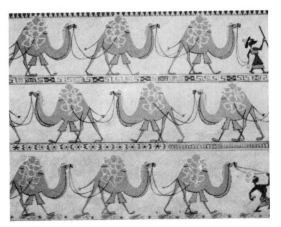

Consider the ancient potter
(And the ancient potter's daughter).
They work with a will
Not only with energy, but with skill,
To make lots
Of pots.
And not only for themselves;
Also, they fill the shelves
Of their neighbours
With the fruits of their labours . . .

*

An endless flow—
Pot after pot!
How do they know
They'll all be bought?
Of course! There must be regions
Wherein dwell legions
Of people, who, being thoughtless,
Find themselves potless.
The camel
Is a useful mammal.
Let us be bold,
And use our hard-earned gold
To invest in one.
Go West on one! –
Into the vast unknown, undaunted,
To find some place where pots are wanted!

*

But will the potter
(And his daughter)
Exploit
The situation? –
Be adroit;
Expand into a large scale organisation
For providing foreigners
In far away corners
With stuff
Of which they haven't enough?
Say,
About
A hundred shekels outlay
On a new layout
Which will put out
Without doubt
An output
Of absolute
Pippins
At threepence
A go
Or so.
Across the desert and the plains
(To distant places
Run by other races)
We'll send our camel trains,
Led by Gideonites, Egyptians, Ancient Greeks and Ancient Gurkhas
Until the desert is as busy as Piccadilly Circus.
By Enterprise
To the skies!

*

Thus, it is clear,
Our Ancient Potter became the pioneer
Of all the Merchant Adventurers . . .
To the Medieval Venetians.
Merchant Adventurers in vast numbers:
Marco Polo – Christopher Columbus –
Sir Walter Ralegh – Cabot – Cooke –
Names you'll find in every history book.
The enterprising!
Who set sail for a far "horizing";
Opening up new areas
For all the various
Commodities
And oddities
That made
World trade,
In those far-off times
And climes.
Let us now turn history's page
And examine our own age –

client's story in an amusing way (like my ancient potter).

Refuse point blank to cover all the really dull stuff like facts and figures in commentary. These can usually be handled much more amusingly when they are tackled graphically.

Remain creatively alive even in the face of the most daunting circumstances. Suppose it is to be a film for the Tea Board. And the fact to be put across is: "Never store tea near any foods which smell strongly".

Commentary might run as follows:

"Now tea is a delicate plant,
So you can't
Mix it in the larder
With things that smell harder"

Not a masterpiece of lyrical poetry, but at least a little less dull than the given fact.

Now for the film which is not sponsored, but aimed purely at the entertainment market. The writer will presumably have ideas for visual treatment and visual gags. These I do not intend to cover. I will treat him purely as a writer of words, words which will be heard either as commentary or dialogue in the finished film.

First, and most important, do not allow yourself to be made to feel like a second class citizen in this world of visual art. You are not. You are just as important as the other fellow worker.

Write him some words which exude humour and atmosphere, wit and gaiety and he'll find himself drawing to your masterpiece.

I know, I've done it.

So, writers of the world, write and write.

10. STORYBOARD FOR ANIMATED FEATURE FILM
Osamu Tezuka (Japan)

The Japanese animation film industry has, during the last ten years, become the largest in the world. Their output has included thirty full length films during that period, five of them directed by Osamu Tezuka.

Mr. Tezuka describes his problems in detail, and we are delighted to show a part of his most elaborate and detailed storyboard for his film: *Thousand and One Nights.*

A few years ago, MUSHI Productions was asked by the Japan Herald Motion Picture Co. Ltd. to produce a full-length animated cartoon film for adult theatre audiences. On that occasion we felt the need for a theoretical analysis of the meaning of animated cartoon films for adults.

Since Walt Disney began making full-length cartoon films, the pattern of the full-length cartoon film seems to have been fairly rigidly set. For one thing, it has become a film aimed at the entertainment of the so-called family audience, an audience composed of children, their parents and adults in their circles, being highly effective for the mobilization of spectators. It is usually a comic story cartoon film woven round an innocent melodrama like a Hollywood entertainment film and spiced with fantasies and humour.

In view of the decline of Hollywood, it was necessary for us to get rid of certain preconceptions about the so-called full-length cartoon feature. But it is more difficult to purge the minds of an audience of that image implanted by Disney. Disney films are released every seven years as new films and continue to draw audiences of considerable size.

Apart from the question of how a new feature animated cartoon film for an adult audience should look, we asked ourselves whether it was possible to draw only adult spectators (including young people) with such a film, whether it would not inevitably draw a family audience composed mainly of children because of the established concept of cartoon films and whether the appraisal of a film based on such a misunderstanding would not deter an audience composed of various age groups.

A number of films clearly directed at an adult audience had been produced in the past—for instance, by Halas & Batchelor Productions (*Animal Farm*) and by Paul Grimault (*La Bergère et le Ramoneur*). But the statistics detailing the age groups of the actual viewers for these films were not available. At the same time, no reports had been heard that *La Bergère et le Ramoneur* had attained any remarkable degree of success. So far as the full-length cartoon film is concerned, it seems safe as a film for the entertainment of children. However, it may require the determination and adventurousness needed for an assault on Mt. Everest to produce a cartoon film for an adult audience.

For what purpose do we produce a cartoon film for an adult audience? It should be to supply adults with fantasies which are disappearing from all forms of entertainment and at the same time to seek the pleasure of motion by returning to the point of departure, the motion picture.

Disney's efforts to seek realism developed into mannerism, but what is entertaining an inexhaustible number of adults in Disneyland is the perfect combination of these two elements. I think the various experimental animated cartoon shorts produced at present by able animators in various countries, including those submitted to film festivals, represent the same thing. So long as we are faithful to the original principle of the motion picture, it should be possible to make a successful adult full-length animated cartoon film. It should make use of the same elements as those employed in a good live-action feature.

When I was asked by the Japan Herald Motion Picture Co. to name a few literary works which might be dramatized in a full-length animated cartoon film for an adult audience my first choice was Goethe's *Faust*. The work's deep philosophy would certainly give satisfaction to adult spectators and at the same time it had, we thought, abundant possibilities for the use of techniques realizable through animation. But the plan was dropped because it was argued that a half-baked adaptation would destroy the value of the original work. As a result, we tackled instead a story from the Middle East. But I did not myself have enough courage to decide positively on the Arabian Nights Entertainment. A large number of animated films had been produced in Hollywood and elsewhere on the same theme, including a masterpiece *The Thief of Baghdad* and what in my opinion was a failure, a film such as the *Thousand and One Nights* (a U.P.A. Magoo film). The public should by that time have had enough of the Arabian Nights' Entertainment. Conversely, the fact that so many films continue to be produced using that work as a basis, we thought, would seem to indicate that it has its particular merits. In building up an original story on the basis of the *Thousand and One Nights*, I considered that the previous films were so freely adapted that they tended to slight or restrict the scope of important main characters (and affairs). The main stories to be taken up by Hollywood are *Aladdin and the Wonderful Lamp*, *Ali Baba and the Forty Thieves* and *Sindbad the Sailor*.

But there are many other captivating main characters in the original stories. If we were to attempt a complete film version of the *Thousand and One Nights* by making use of all these characters, we thought, we might be able to produce a very substantial film.

IN SEARCH OF A HERO

At the same time, to interrelate these episodes which were to be introduced in an omnibus style, it would be necessary to create a protagonist who would link separate stories together. And the leading character must behave as an adult, must have the personality of an adult and must act in a way fully persuasive to the ideology or theme of the film.

After several long discussions with my staff, I set the theme of the film as a search for eternal youth, vitality and the frontier spirit. I wanted to model the hero after some contemporary personalities who are tough, dauntless, adequately mercenary and shrewd and who aspire to be successful through intelligence and audacity rather than through physical prowess. While I was hunting for a film star at the festivals in Hollywood and elsewhere, who would provide the image of the character we needed, my eyes lighted on Jean-Paul Belmondo. And as I studied his personality, even the face of the film character began to take after Belmondo's. It verged on being a portrait, but it served to give the exact image of the hero to my staff.

The story was woven round the wonderings of the hero Aldin. We thought we should avoid as much as possible the stories concerning princes and princesses, which were a worn out old trick of the conventional entertainment film. A vagabond, nameless, poor, powerless, but eloquent was the role allotted to the leading character. As a common man of today is threatened by politics, oppressed by large enterprises and suffering from modern diseases, so our hero was persecuted to the extreme and was even deprived of his sweetheart. By describing this tragedy in a comic vein, we contrived a situation in which the audience might feel empathy with the hero. This made it necessary to present a villain who symbolised various modern evils, to contrast with him.

The villain should neither be a man of simple character as the leader of the forty thieves, nor the malicious minister who invariably crosses swords with the hero at a climax. He should have as complex a mind and as strong a character as the hero. His human image as the rival must win the belief of the spectators.

As an important villain we created Badli. He is a Machiavellian. If the hero Aldin is positive, he is negative; he is a character who has the same ideal as the hero's though taking the opposite direction in life. Pretending to be constantly loyal to the ruler, he commits opportunistic betrayal cold-bloodedly; his final goal in life is to seize absolute power, but he never stands in front and takes full responsibility. He is a cunning and wily character.

The two characters must be in constant opposition throughout the stories. The hero Aldin pursued his in a capricious way. To this end, he would thoughtlessly throw away accumulated fortune and acquired position. The very thing coveted by Badli was to the hero Aldin almost worthless once it had been won.

It was not so difficult to surround these two main characters with a bevy of minor figures. Milliam, the heroine, whom Aldin continued to love and who was to be killed by Badli; Jallis, a daughter of Aldin and Milliam, but whom Aldin did not know to be his own daughter; Kamhakim, the leader of a robber band whom Badli made use of to gain power; Madia, the daughter of Kamhakim, who despised the villain and who was raped by him; Aslan, the lover of Jallis, who was a shepherd. All these characters were introduced to set off the two main characters. The hero Aldin is a water-vendor in the original. We only borrowed his name; he is a different character from the famous Aladdin of the wonderful lamp. But because Aladdin was so popular, we received many enquiries about our possibly having meant Aladdin when we used the name Aldin. In fact, when our film was first shown to film distributors of various nations, they all asked this same question. But those who are well versed in the original may understand that all the names of the characters who appear in this film are the names of those who appear in various episodes of the original.

The various famous scenes of the Arabian Nights' Entertainment were effectively fitted into the progress of our story. The "Open Sesame" cave, the flying wooden horse, the isle of women, the woman who is an incarnation of a snake, the Rop-rop bird, the Cyclops, the ghost ship—all these could be integrated into the story of Aldin's wanderings.

HUMOUR

Another element which could not be missing from an animated film is humour in the form of gag as well as images. We provided this in abundance, and to enhance the effects of scenes, we introduced Gin and his wife Ginie on the stage, a married couple in an episode in the original work. Gin, at the turning-point of matrimonial life and a capricious middle-aged husband, is under the control of his wife, Ginie, who is jealous, shrewd and desirous of falling in love with someone else. We thought that the humour produced by the couple as they practised magic would add brightness and colour to the main story, which might otherwise become gloomy and argumentative.

PROBLEMS AND CUTS

Thus, a story composed of colourful characters and plots developed into a scenario extending to over 3 hours 50 minutes. The story was divided into three parts: in Part I, Aldin is persecuted by Badli, his loved one is killed and he starts on a journey as Sindbad the sailor; in Part II, Sindbad returns to the capital and becomes king by the power of his fortune; and in Part III, King Aldin reaches a confrontation with Badli, leaves the throne and begins another journey.

Osamu Tezuka
Part of visual story continuity from
Thousand and one Nights from Japan.

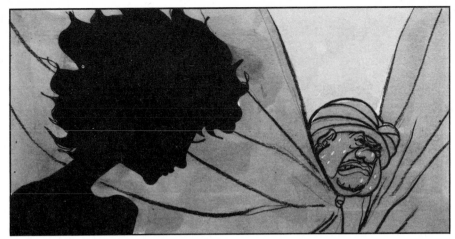

Except for Aldin, Jallis and Aslan, all the colourful characters die. Death has seldom been depicted in animated cartoons. To show the death of a character with violence or murder has always been taboo. It was a test for us to break the taboo.

After repeated examinations, we shortened the scenario to 2 hours 30 minutes and started our operation using that as the basis. The completed film was still lengthy, extending over 2 hours 28 minutes, so with possible spectator fatigue in mind, we inserted an intermission.

Such a lengthy cartoon film has not been attempted even by Walt Disney. But mere length has nothing to do with how substantial the film's content is.

The distribution company lodged the complaint that a cartoon film requiring 2 hours 30 minutes for showing was a box office risk and proposed that it be cut to 2 hours for presentation in the theatre. With deep regret I deleted a number of episodes to shorten the film by 20 minutes. In animation terms, the deletion amounted to 15,000 pictures, a great disappointment to the animators and painters.

The print finally completed took 2 hours 9 minutes to show—probably the longest animated film ever produced.

The animated pictures used amounted to 160,000. In about a year and a half, from the start of the project to its completion, 600,000 man-days were required. (The revision for foreign distribution was shortened by another 30 minutes, which necessitated a minor revision of the story and a weakening of the characterization of the hero Aldin. To our regret the deletion of the Rop-rop Bird, the Cyclops, the desert and the woods scenes made the continuity of the story somewhat clumsy. All those films sent to England and other countries are the shortened revision).

The film, publicised as the first animated cartoon film for adult entertainment, attracted a 3 million, mainly youthful audience in Japan in the first six months—a great success and well beyond our expectations.

But as we had invested an enormous sum of money in the production, this success brought only a meagre profit. We must now pin our hopes on proceeds from abroad and the results of showing a new version. On the heels of this film, we produced another full-length cartoon film for adults, *Cleopatra*. This was followed by a screen version of *Faust*, in an original arrangement.

THE IMPORTANCE OF THE SCRIPT

The lesson we have learned from producing these films is that no matter how excellent a film is pictorially, no matter how superb in animation technique, and no matter how good in eliciting laughter, what decides its fortune is the synopsis and scenario. Whereas children see animation merely for the sake of the pleasure of motion, and burst into laughter at cunning gags, the present audience in the 'youth' age group seek some food for thought from a film or want to theorize on it. In the interest of such people, a full-length cartoon film should have a scenarios representing a solid and colourful story. The day has gone when it is possible to attract a large audience with a film which is merely entertaining, amusing and beautiful.

The problem of finance in film production can be formidable. The cost of a professionally produced live feature film is seldom under $1,000,000 and it could be considerably more. In order to earn back such money a film must gross more than double this sum at the box office. In case of the animated feature the expenditure could be higher as the time of making a film is much longer. Many animated films take two or three years to make, and the cost of labour (often 60 to 100 artists and technicians involved) can be of several million dollars.

One way to economise and to cut costs without substantially effecting the quality of the film is to prepare the storyboard in great detail, and to simplify the production process carefully. A live action director can depend on his star performer for the delivery of a line, the dramatisation of the dialogue and the action. He can also depend on his lighting cameraman and camera operator to record the performances onto film. The instant contribution of human elements is essential for any live production. In animation such contribution is carried out by the key animators and their assistants, tracers and painters, who follow through the animation onto celluloids, the background artist providing the scenery and the cameraman who photograph the assembled work film frame by film frame. Unless each step is co-ordinated in a progressive and logical order, an enormous amount of time could be wasted and the budget badly unbalanced. A further consideration is given to the degree of animation density. Whether an action demands 24 frames per second or 12 frames only is an important decision which a director has to make. On this depends not only how smooth the animation will appear on the screen but how expensive the film will be. The more animated drawing employed the more tracing and painting follow up will be required, and also more time under the camera. Usually there are several celluloid levels for each individual shot, each level of celluloid representing only the moving part of a figure while another level holds statically such part which does not require movement. Also when more than one figure animates in a shot others may be held motionless on a static celluloid. The manipulation of these levels could affect the amount of work and consequently the expenditure of that shot. Only an experienced director knows the best way to combine the celluloid levels for the best effect.

Additional consideration should be given to the outline of an animated figure. If it is too complex it will take a very long time to draw, and may not be the most effective way to express whatever movement such a figure is required to do. Simplicity of outline often is the most effective and economical approach in an animated feature. The number of colours on a character could be also an expensive item in a film. The early Disney films often had 12 to 18 colours on a figure. Today,

seven colours are the most. The rich textures of early cartoons are replaced by bolder graphic design, which in a way could be just as effective.

The director has, in fact, a considerable control over the many processes that affect the final shape, density, look of a film and with such a control he also has a decisive role in the budget. An expenditure of $1,000,000 could be reduced considerably by careful planning.

This is what John Wilson has attempted to achieve in his film *Shinbone Alley*. His storyboard for this film (original title *Archy and Mehitabel*) is an excellent example of an approach which uses economically planned animation to the full, while remaining very close to the original material. The film story is taken from the Broadway play, *Archy and Mehitabel* by Don Marquis. It is about Archy, the cockroach who writes poems by jumping on to keys of a typewriter.

The voice of Archy was Eddie Bracken, who had played the part on Broadway and Carol Channing was chosen as Mehitable the cat.

An intelligent inspired storyboard can save 30–50 per cent of a budget, and the audience is not even aware of such cutbacks. In some cases a less laboured film is the result, with a more skilled and flowing story.

John Wilson the director of *Shinbone Alley* describes his method for a budget feature production.

The essence of the animated film is the storyboard, sketch layout, and 'setup' approach to the picture. Once the concept is fairly conceived and developed (and no two concepts can be handled in an identical way), it should be exhaustively explored as to the graphic statement desired. This has been my experience—that the original idea, story concept, whatever, is the motivating force of the whole picture, and should be adhered to right to the cut work-print stage. The director, once having seen the desired goal in his mind, should not deviate from this goal. This is the discipline required. There are many temptations, suggestions and alternatives, and each should be considered carefully. If it enhances or adds to the dimensions of the overall statement, it can be considered—otherwise ruthlessly discarded. In this manner, it is possible for the director to 'see' his finished film completed in his mind's eye, and watch the final picture completing itself physically on time and within budget.

ECONOMICS

There are five areas of animated film production, which are separate and distinct, yet economically interdependent. These are:

1 Storyboard; 3 Layout and Background Painting; 3 Animation; 4 Ink and Paint; 5 Camera.

If careful *consideration* is given to these from the outset (that is at concept and development stage) there is less likelihood of one department getting out of hand in terms of time, money or control.

If the storyboard is thoroughly developed, the sketch layouts carefully prepared and the colour models on cel in exactly the right way, a firm production continuity can be forecast accurately. This may seem to be a simple obvious fact, but it is surprising how many pictures do not get completed because they were not thought out properly at the beginning.

An animated feature film is a major undertaking and a strenuous exercise in mental stamina, both for the producer and the audience. All drawings in frame by frame continuity are a mental exercise, since a drawing *is* a mental exercise. "If you can think it, you can animate it" is my rule in making pictures.

SHINBONE ALLEY PRODUCTION METHODS

As this picture was a 'musical' it had to have colour, life and full animation, and a depth of experience that equalled the writing of Don Marquis.

Each of the five production divisions mentioned had to be considered as a function that could be performed once and once only, due to the limitations of budget.

John Wilson
Carol Channing is transformed to animated cat constructed for simplified animation from the film *Shinbone Alley*.

STORYBOARD

Three storymen and a director worked with the composer and screenwriter for a period of three months in order to arrive at the total continuity of story, dialogue, music and mood. The flow of continuity was considered as a high priority, and when the storyline was approved, the storymen were able to rough sketch the character reaction, dialogue, humour etc. until movement and mood were smooth and interwoven. This was when the mood sketches and emotional involvement with the characters were set. It is at this precise moment, that the director has to 'see' the sequence completed in his mind. At this stage (the completion of all the other sequences), the group of storymen, writer and composer were disbanded. The director now had a completed score, libretto, screenplay and storyboard. He had to seclude himself and time out the entire length of the feature, make changes, draw character setups for difficult personality statements. This took about a month using the minimum of staff whose task was to organise recording sessions, call in actors for casting, and arrange contracts and production schedules. Not until all these steps had been carried out were the layout artists and designers hired.

RECORDING

By very careful attention to detail, all 310 music cues were broken down into musical groupings—the solo songs, the duet, the full orchestra, the small orchestra, etc. By this method, and by pre-recording the orchestra, we were able to record all cues, both voice and music, in about fifteen working days. The competence of an excellent music director and manager made this possible. From these sync-pulse eight-track tapes, the entire soundtrack of *Shinbone Alley* was assembled again, once and once only. No pick-ups or re-recording were necessary, although the entire picture was constructed from these cues by an animation editor after photography was complete. At this time, it was his arbitary use and choice of the music cues that ended up on the screen.

LAYOUT AND DESIGN

Five layout men (planning sketches and models) now began to set the stage and, again, every note, every mood and every line of dialogue was staged for the animators. Their period of employment lasted the full six months of animation in order to accommodate the director's work with the animators. Background artists were also employed for the whole time in order to give full range to the graphic possibilities of each sequence. For instance, colour models were drawn for every line of the 'Ladybugs of the Evening' sequence, which became one of the most important sections of the film. Artists were cast according to their ability, one artist being responsible for the overall appearance of the picture—and reflect the earthy, tenuous, ascetic philosophy of the original author, Don Marquis.

ANIMATION

The director personally interpreted each sequence to each animator, again casting the animator specifically in a role which suited him best. Approximately thirty animators, producing thirty feet of animation a week each, worked for four months making full animation drawings. Personal interpretation was encouraged. Personality development and character movement were communicated to all assistants during this period.

INK AND PAINT

Full checking and production co-ordination by three checkers made it possible to pass all animation to a Xerox to machine trace the drawings, and 'paint' with minimum confusion, in preparation for the camera.

One camera, working two shifts, enabled shooting to be completed on schedule (about four months) with careful planning overlapping the animation, ink and paint work. Apart from the character models, no pencil tests were shot for any of the production, this saving money, and cutting out one stage from the routine production method. At the laboratory, tests were made to allow rush prints of individual shots to be made on one light. This enabled the director to control the final image immediately at minimum expense. Retakes for restaging or colour correction were thus held to the minimum for the entire 10,000 feet of film shot. Editing and sound effects took three weeks, and dubbing the final track to picture took five days.

ADDITIONAL COMMENTS

Premises were rented to enable the entire production to be made under one roof. A team spirit thus developed that made its own comfortable pattern of delivery speed. This is not always necessary, but if the entire production is not taken carefully into consideration at the beginning and at the end of every week of work, the producer is risking disaster, economically and artistically.

'Bug' one of the leading characters in *Shinbone Alley*. Only four colours are used instead of twelve, yet it is still colourful.

Background design for *Shinbone Alley*. Expressive and powerful graphic design can be less costly than over-laboured backgrounds.

12. COMBINED LIVE ACTION/CARTOON FEATURE FILM

Gunnar Karlson (Sweden)

Although animation is a small part of the film industry it has been an important section of it on account of its high creativity and technical experiments. Throughout the years many new ideas in cinematography emerged from the animation industry; like multiplane photography, colour coding, speed timing, hold frames, aerial image photography, and some aspects of double exposure to name a few. The same cannot be maintained the other way round, as yet. The two media—live and animated—however, differ substantially in several respects. The two major differences are first the production method, second their effect on audiences.

LIVE-CARTOONS AND AUDIENCE EFFECT

Live action is a reproductive process based primarily on natural speed as action develops in reality; animation is based on sequential progression whereby the action is advanced by changing each individual frame slightly. The internal production organisation has to be different too, and must be conditioned by the performances dictated by the technique itself. The effect of live photography is a reflection of reality often enlarged by the camera to create a dramatic illusion. Animation on the other hand, attempts to depart from reality, and establish its own imaginary world, and since it is drawn by hand the characters as well as the backgrounds become symbols. It is essential that these elements should be highly simplified. Here is the reason why the two levels do not mix naturally. They also demand a different level of time development. Natural speed appears far too slow for animation as the simplified characters and background allow for a speedier audience perception. Cartoon speed appears unnatural if superimposed over a live-action scene.

The two techniques need a most careful balance which may be the reason why so few combined live plus cartoon animation films have been produced until the present time. The Swedish experiments by Gunnar Karlson and Per Åhlin opens up the whole question of relationship once more. The Swedish feature length *Dunderklumpen* provides some elements of new ideas of how the problem should be approached and solved. The producer Gunnar Karlson describes his experience on the subject.

Some years ago the world of full length films in Sweden, which averages twenty productions a year, saw the birth of a surprising child. Called *Out of an Old Man's Head,* it was in a format entirely new to the Swedish film industry—a full length animated film with short live sequences. This format resulted from the content of the script —an old man in an old people's home (live action) remembering and fantasising about his past (animation). However, although it received the approval of the Swedish Film Institute, and more than covered its costs on the domestic market, the critics did not show very much understanding of what the film was about. Amusing and entertaining on the one hand, it also had touches of melancholy which were not fully appreciated, and so it has led to a new venture which aims to use the live and cartoon combination in a more readily appreciable way, and which is the main subject of this article.

The production of *Out of an Old Man's Head* was the most ambitious project in the history of GK film, which was formed in 1953, and is the only company in Sweden to work continuously with animated film. Over the years, advertising films, television spots, television films, puppet films and commercials for foreign countries have been produced. The move to feature length production came from the desire to expand the range of the company with something out of the ordinary, and thanks to the co-operation of the artist Per Åhlin it was possible to realise this plan.

Per Åhlin co-directed, designed and animated the film and was largely responsible for its success. The experience gained from it has resulted in a project under the working title of *The Enchanted People*—a full length film intended as family entertainment, but with the children as a point of departure. Per Ahlin directs it, and it has a production schedule of three years.

COMBINED LIVE/CARTOON PRODUCTION

In *The Enchanted People*, the role of visual writer is shared between the members of a small team, so that the talents and skills needed for writing for this medium will emerge by implication rather than by an attempt to define what is required of a particular individual. It is to be hoped that the methods and requirements of this film can act as a potential model for combined media film productions of all types—between live film and all the various types of animation, video and computer techniques as and when the possibilities emerge in the rapidly-expanding technology of the present era.

This particular mixture of live action and cartoon is in itself nothing new. The technique has been used in several films by Disney and is often utilised in different kinds of advertising film. But it has never before been used to this extent in Europe.

THE MEDIUM

Where *Out of an Old Man's Head* relied on the contrast between completely live and completely animated sequences to supply both pathos and humour, *The Enchanted People* project is aiming for a subtler approach, and using trick techniques to combine live and animated characters on the screen simultaneously. In addition to ordinary scenes with 'living' actors, there are sequences in which the animated figures move in live surround-

Per Åhlin
Part of the storyboard of Gunnar Karlson's *Dunderklumpen*. Produced by GK-Film Studio (pages 101-105).

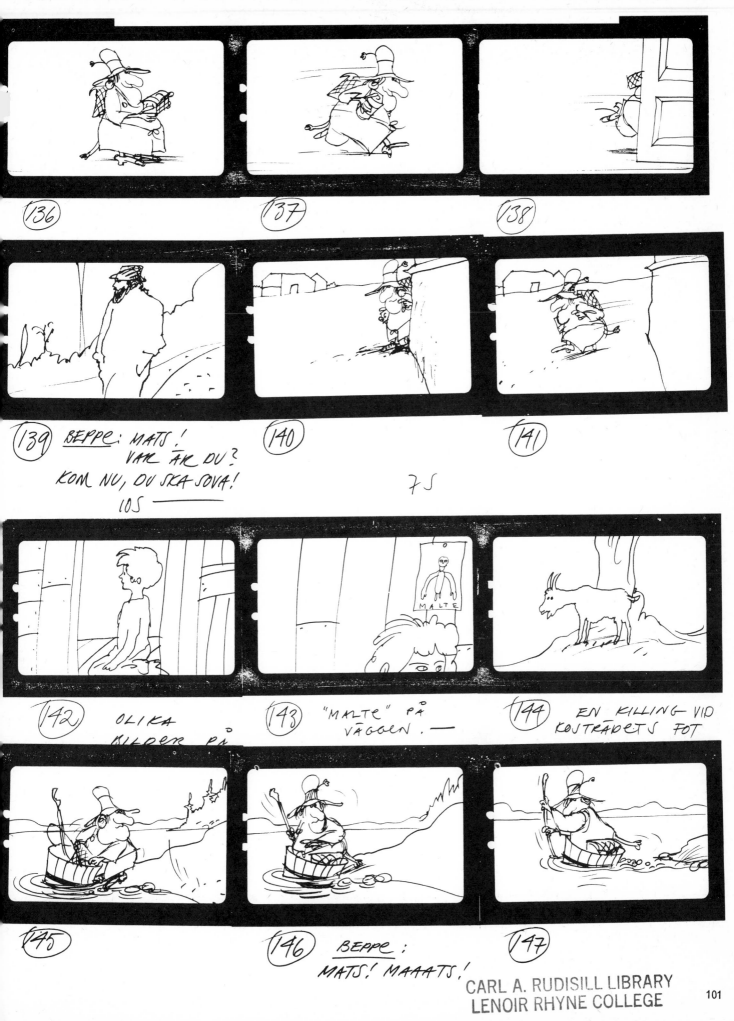

136

137

138

139 BEPPE: MATS!
VAR ÄR DU?
KOM NU, DU SKA SOVA!
10S ———

140

141

75

142 OLIKA
BILDER PÅ

143 "MALTE" PÅ
VÄGGEN. ——

144 EN KILLING VID
KOSTRÄDETS FOT

145

146 BEPPE:
MATS! MAAATS!

147

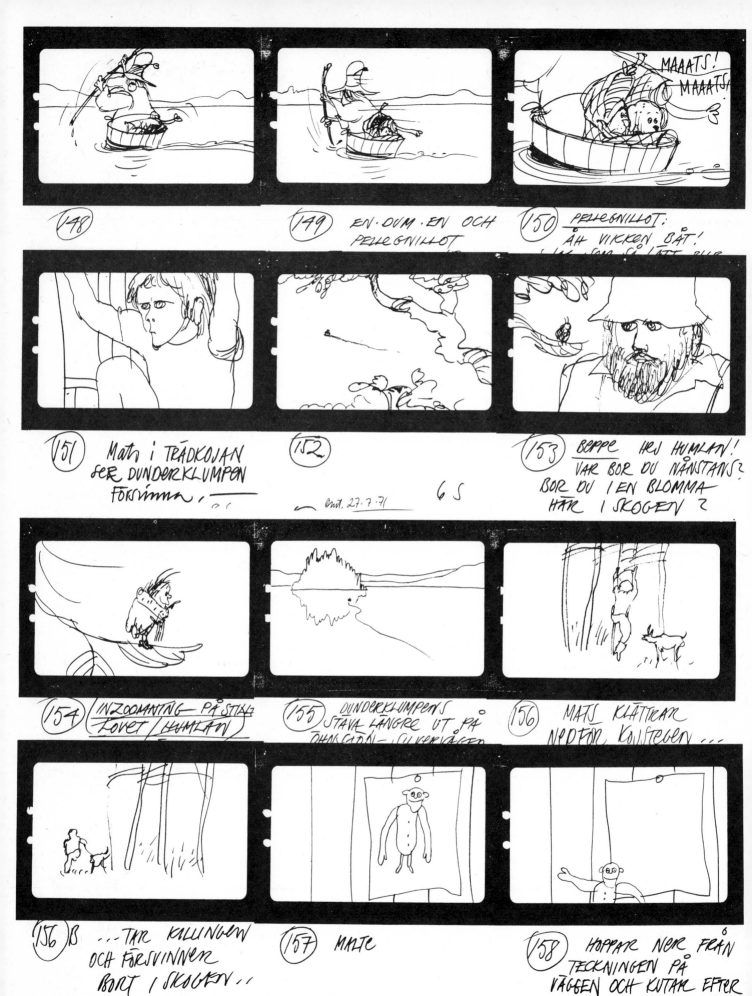

148

149 EN · OUM · EN OCH
PELLEGNILLOT

150 PELLEGNILLOT:
ÄH VIKKEN BÅT!

151 Mats i TRÄDKOJAN
ser DUNDERKLUMPEN
försvinna. ——

152 ~ Ont. 27·7·71   6 S

153 BEPPE HEJ HUMLAN!
VAR BOR DU NÅNSTANS?
BOR DU I EN BLOMMA
HÄR I SKOGEN ?

154 INZOOMNING PÅ STIG
LÖVET / HUMLAN

155 DUNDERKLUMPENS
STAVA LÄNGRE UT PÅ
ÖHNSIÖN — SILVERVÄGEN

156 MATS KLÄTTRAR
NEDFÖR KONSTEGEN ...

156 B ... TAR KILLINGEN
OCH FÖRSVINNER
BORT I SKOGEN ..

157 MALTE

158 HOPPAR NER FRÅN
TECKNINGEN PÅ
VÄGGEN OCH KUTAR EFTER
MATS OCH KILLINGEN —

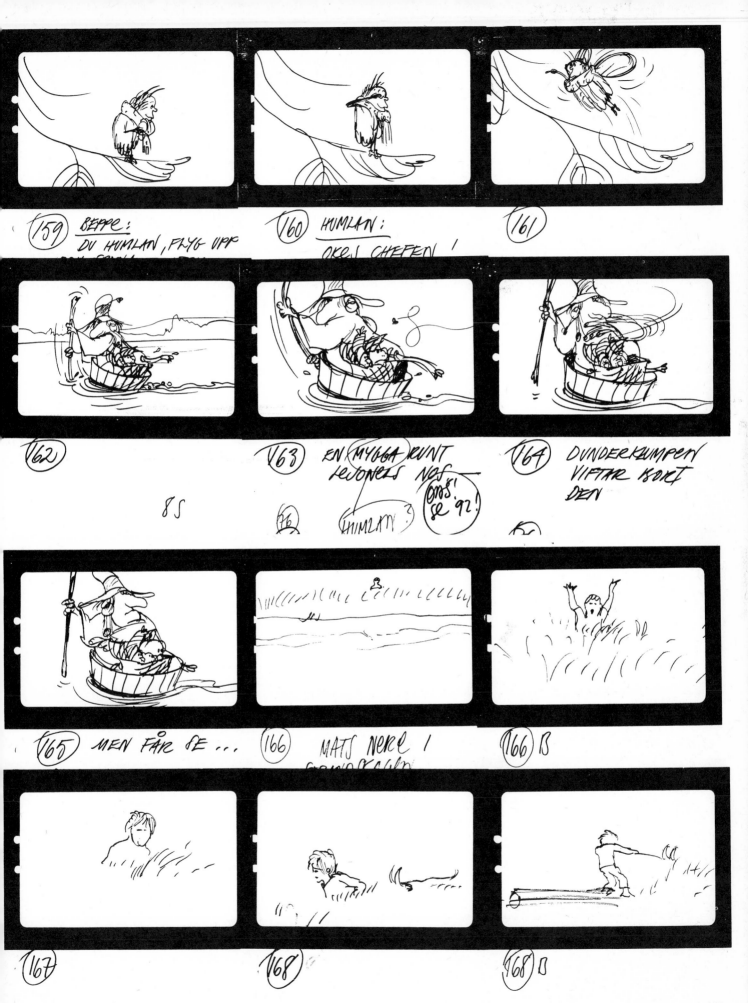

159 BEPPE:
DU HUMLAN, FLYG UPP

160 HUMLAN:
OKEJ CHEFEN!

161

162

8 S

163 EN MYGGA RUNT
LEJONETS NOS

164 DUNDERKLUMPEN
VIFTAR BORT
DEN

165 MEN FÅR SE...

166 MATS NERE I
GRÄSDÄLEN

166 B

167

168

168 B

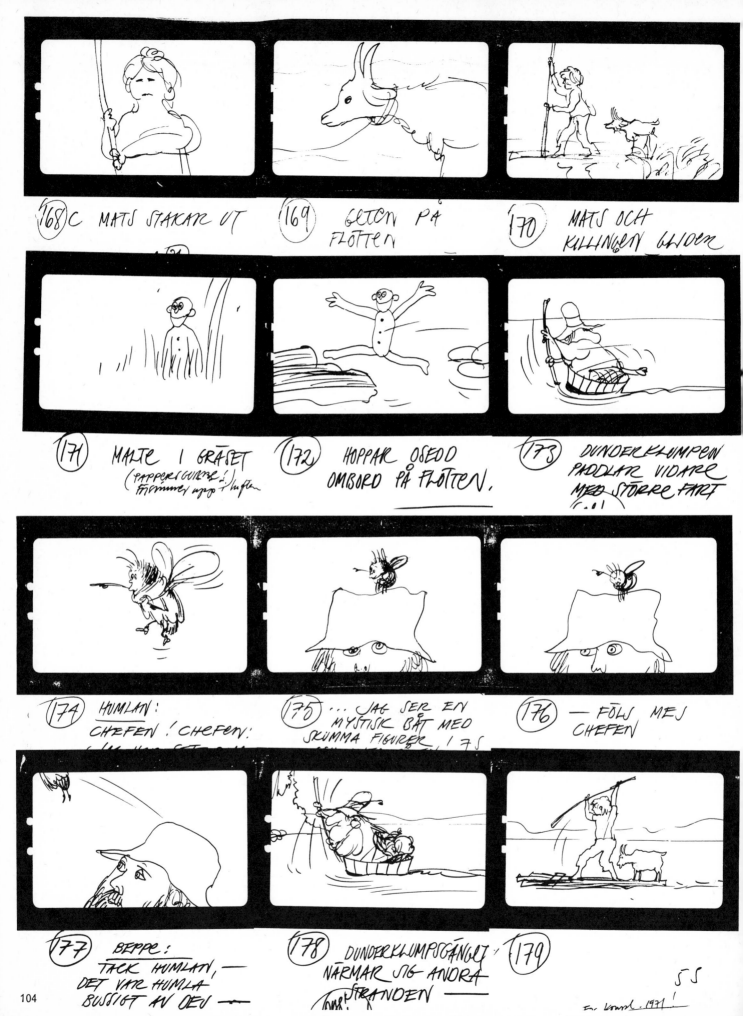

168 C MATS STAKAR UT

169 GETEN PÅ FLOTTEN

170 MATS OCH KILLINGEN GLIDER

171 MALTE I GRÄSET (PAPPERSGUBBE!) främmer upp i luften

172 HOPPAR OSEDD OMBORD PÅ FLOTTEN.

173 DUNDERKLUMPEN PADDLAR VIDARE MED STÖRRE FART (...)

174 HUMLAN: CHEFEN! CHEFEN!

175 ... JAG SER EN MYSTISK BÅT MED SKUMMA FIGURER. 175

176 — FÖLJ MEJ CHEFEN

177 BEPPE: TACK HUMLAN, — DET VAR HUMLA BUSSIGT AV DEJ —

178 DUNDERKLUMPSGÄNGET NÄRMAR SIG ANDRA STRANDEN —

179

55

En. brand. 1971

104

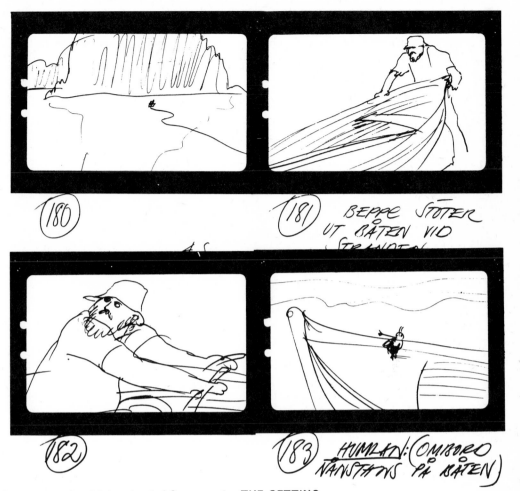

180

181 BEPPE STÖTER
UT BÅTEN VID
STRANDEN

182

183 HUMLAN: (OMBORD
NÄNSTANS PÅ BÅTEN)

ings and sequences in which animated figures act together with living actors.

There are also scenes which are wholly animated.

THE SCRIPT

The first manuscript draft is written by a well-known children's entertainer whose speciality is song texts. The project is then fully discussed between director and writer, and later the visual possibilities are pinpointed, both from an artistic and from a technical point of view. The result is a final script from which is constructed a storyboard—unusually detailed, with about 1400 continuity story sketches which cover the completely live sequences as well as the rest. The storyboard changes radically as the live shooting (which is done first) reveals new problems and ideas.

THE MUSIC

As in the case of most animated films, the music has to be finished before the artist can set to work. In this film the music is very important, and during the whole process of production close co-operation between composer, artist-director and lyrics writer is a must. The film contains several sequences in which the characters sing, play and dance.

THE SETTING

The choice of location plays a large part in fixing the film's mood and helping to overcome technical difficulties. An island in the north of Sweden, with forests, mountains, rapids and waterfalls, is the live background in which the film's actors live. The aim is to make full use of nature and the Swedish midsummer night, when hobgoblins and fairies traditionally come to life. Realism can be mixed with fantasy to form a genre which draws strongly on Swedish folklore.

The crew often has to wait for cloudy weather. It is needed to bring out the unreal light which comes from the midnight sun and is so characteristic of summer nights in north Sweden. It also makes the picture less three-dimensional so that the flat animated characters melt better into the complete product, and it enables the use of a subdued saturated range of colours.

THE PLOT

A small, round, animated figure, called Dunderlumpken climbs in through a window and steals a boy's toys: doll, teddy bear, the smallest lion in the world, a hare-like figure wrapped in a pyjama jacket and a treasure chest. A child's drawing—Malte—goes along too, and they all become alive, i.e., animated figures. From here on, the film

The finished art work from Gunnar
Karlson's *Dunderklumpen*.

The final effect combining live shots with cartoon.

consists of a complicated chase, punctuated by meetings with various fairy beings. The boy chases his escaped toys, his father and the family goat chase him. A bumble bee functions as messenger and scout, and an evil creature called One-Eye is the villain of the piece who causes confusion to the humans by his ability to make banknotes at will.

THE VIEWPOINT

Many of today's comics and cartoons idolise making money, growing up big and strong, and being best at everything. *The Enchanted People* attempts another emphasis. The aim is to make a film that is both funny and entertaining but which excludes all forms of sadism, violence and frightening episodes. It makes fun of various prejudices and generally promotes the idea that there are ways of life that work better than the rat race. To do this without being stuffy and obvious is one of the most challenging problems in the film.

LIVE SHOOTING

Equally challenging are the technical problems. The ultimate responsibility for these lies with the director, but a project like this is only possible if he has wide-ranging experience in other fields. Per Åhlin, born in 1931, has been an animator, cartoonist, commercial artist, scenographer and photographer as well as a director for both stage and film. The combined live action-cartoon film requires all these skills, both in technical versatility and in artistic visualising power. In *Out of an Old Man's Head*, Åhlin worked over the script, led the live shooting, and created the animated characters.

For the new film, he has also to mix the two types of characters, and background in the same picture, and he carries out a good deal of precision work on his own.

The actors work in accordance with the director's instructions. All the animated figures' scenes, which will later be copied in, exist only in his head, and for him it is a complex matter of making them come alive for the actors. This can be very complex as it is also dependent on exact timing. The rhythm must be fixed beforehand, and as far as the actors are concerned it is not only a question of their getting an idea of their own way of functioning, but also of how the "invisible actor" functions in the picture. The actor has to act together with a non-existent being, realised for him in terms of the director's powers of imagination so that the character is seen and almost known. Real objects which are to move as a result of the actions of the animated characters must be set in motion by various tricks. As the work progresses the director must find ingenious solutions.

Everything must then act in concert so that the animated characters fuse with the dramatic action of the film.

THE ANIMATION

There are about ten animated characters in the film, and they are worked out in detail far in advance, before the actual production is started. The plot of the film, on the other hand, is not fixed in every detail. This leaves room for improvisation and changes during the course of the work. The first live shooting results in a number of changes in, and additions to, the original storyboard, which suggests a rhythm more like a live-action entertainment film than an animated cartoon.

This rhythm is very important if a film of this sort is to function. The mixture of cartoon and live action must feel meaningful; the living actors and the animated must have a chance of meeting; the animated sequences must sometimes grow out of the photographed, sometimes the opposite— all this is to ensure that the story will function in a dramatically credible way.

THE MATTE

The superimposition of the animated characters on the live action scene can be made in different ways, either by using the travelling-matte method or through the technique of the aerial image. In this particular film it was decided to use the method which is regarded as the safest today and most tested in the case of full-length films— travelling matte.

There are different methods of using travelling matte, but the principle is to leave unexposed that part of the live image where the opaqued animated character will appear. The live image now has a hole in it, called a female matte. The exact outlines of the animated character are then printed onto another roll of film, which is otherwise unexposed (this is a male matte), and the two images are finally brought together. This work must be done on an optical printer.

With the aerial image method, the same result can be achieved in another way, with its accompanying problems. This method has, unfortunately, as yet several drawbacks which can be difficult to overcome. The principle behind the aerial image method is to project the live action scene from below, via a special projector and mirror, while at the same time the animated opaqued character is photographed from above, with conventional top lighting and a rostrum camera.

THE TEAM

The number of people working on this project is minute by American production house standards, and from an international point of view it may seem wholly unrealistic to believe that the small group working on the film can achieve its goal. But there are many cases in which a small production team has done as well or better than a giant studio, given the limitations within which it has to work.

If one's judgement of high quality depends on technical perfection then Per Åhlin's film may not meet the required standards. But in his opinion, artistry can never be replaced by technique. He finds it advantageous to work with a small team as the film is given a personal touch and the result should have a spontaneity which should add to its artistic quality and make it more alive. The various trick methods must not become ends in themselves. Technique is solely used to carry the story forward and to transform the mixture of fantasy and reality into a credible unreality.

THE ROLE OF COMBINED
LIVE ACTION/CARTOON FILM

There are several reasons for films to be regularly made in this medium, for it can be of great benefit to animation and to the cinema as a whole.

One is to make a contribution to the further development of animated film in situations where fully animated feature films are too difficult or expensive. A surprisingly small amount of animated film has been made in Sweden, for instance, though it is a country which otherwise has produced several important film makers and films.

Then there is a great need all over the world for films in which imagination and fantasy can provide entertainment which does not rely on sadism and violence. But full-length animated films can sometimes be tiring and not only for adult audiences. This type of animated film with its combination of live and cartoon should be more stimulating to watch. It gives the audience a better chance of identifying with the "living" actors and realistic surroundings. The switches between cartoon and live should be regarded as tricks, but be justified in order to give the plot an added dimension.

Animation and special effects in various forms have a good chance of enriching conventional film, perhaps giving it hitherto unexplored possibilities of renewing itself. And this is worth striking a blow for. The magic possibilities of the moving picture have somehow been denied to most films. It is as though one may only use one's imaginative powers legitimately for children.

This means that combined-media films can be seen as a protest against the fact that the possibilities of animated film have often been underestimated. Small production teams can show that the "factory-made" approach in Disney's style is unnecessary. All over the world carton films are being made by small groups who wish to put a personal stamp on their products, but they are rarely able to reach a mass audience. And animation is the most time-consuming technique in cinema. The uniqueness of the live/cartoon combination lies in the fact that it enables a small team to make a full-length film in the "Disney format", a production for general release in the cinema.

Another protest is involved here. No one can dispute what Disney has meant for the animated film as a form or art—for better or for worse. Neither can anyone dispute the effect of what has been done in reaction against the Disney convention—for better or worse. Unfortunately, the result has been many new conventions which are just as deplorable as the worst of Disney. A change can, quite naturally, only be brought about by those artists and producers who can fight the Disney convention on its own ground, without reproducing the cliché of those artists who have established opposing styles. Here the relatively unexplored territory of films in combined media can offer a real possibility. It is up to the artists and producers to change the attitude that the form of art in question can function solely as TV-spots or as entertainment for children. And this is where the film critic must become aware of his responsibilities and acquire the knowledge of this particular form of filmic art which is dictated by progress.

Experience in Sweden has shown that neither technical nor commercial difficulties need stand in the way of full-length live/cartoon production. The main task of a visual writer for this medium lies in being able to gear his imagination to these considerations when producing a storyboard. He must rid himself of the preconception that animation and live action films are necessarily distinct and incompatible, and instead think of ways in which the two forms can draw strength from each other. When a sufficient number of people are able to think in this way, the combination live/cartoon has every chance of taking its place in the film production of the future.

13. THE EXPERIMENTAL FILM MAKER AND DESIGNER

Norman McLaren (Canada)
Saul Bass (U.S.A.)

One of the advantages which cinematography offers the contemporary artist and designer is movement.

Until the beginning of this century, the artist or visualiser had to content himself solely with using static images to express himself. Movement in a painting or sculpture had to be expressed artificially and could only be symbolic.

Paintings or sculptures of, say, a galloping horse or dancing figures could only be held in frozen attitudes.

In the early days of the cinema, from 1920 onwards, several artists, among them Deschamp and Fischinger, became preoccupied with the 'kinetic' aspect of pictorial composition and tried to express and interpret these elements in motion.

More artists gradually came to recognise that the transitional movement from one attitude to another can be the most important aspect of art, and from this grew a new expression in cinema— the abstract experimental film.

Transitional movement and the metamorphosis from one shape to another was experimented with in many early films by artists such as Leger, Alexeieff and Eggerling and the results showed great vitality.

Today, thousands of film makers are practising this approach; possibly the best known are Norman McLaren and Saul Bass. The early experimental abstract films, for instance Fischinger's *Hungarian Rhapsody* (1931) and Len Lye's *Trade Tattoo* (1932) stirred many of the critics into declaring that this was cinema in its purest form.

This holds true today, although the facilities for creating motion and the possibilities of providing richer textural visual content are naturally now more sophisticated.

The computer has also added new possibilities of expression, as well as reducing tedious routine tasks in production.

At the other end of the scale there is the production of television commercials and animated film titles which have a different objective.

Saul Bass is one of the foremost exponents in this line of production. Norman McLaren's films, although not carried out spontaneously like Sistiaga's are also painted on to the film stock, but with a far more deliberate production plan.

The unifying aspect of most abstract films based on visual continuity, is the dominance and impact of the motion itself, and the attainment of the full potential relationship between colour, harmony, motion and sound.

Movement becomes the most important aspect or the central theme of a film. The sound, whether music or effects, is also used as an integral part of the motion continuity helping to emphasise and accentuate it.

Story development or dialogue is not recognised as an essential element. Movement itself becomes the theme.

Norman McLaren

Sequences from one of the best McLaren films *Blinkety Blank*.

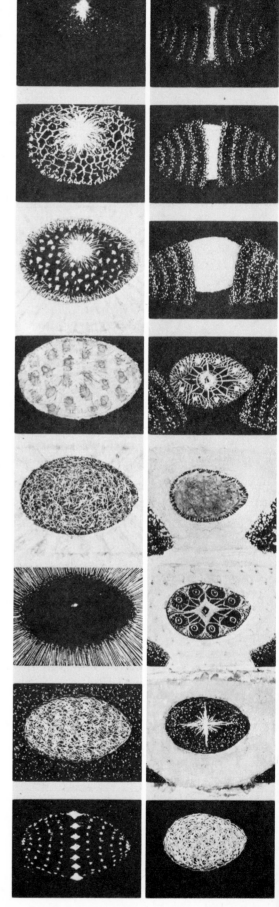

From one of Norman McLaren's latest films *Spheres*,

NORMAN McLAREN

Norman McLaren has a special place in the world of abstract films, not only because of the excellent achievements of his numerous films, but also because of the simple production method he uses to maintain close individual control over every stage of development. He is a one-man unit, typical in abstract film production which requires unity and the personal touch of the artist. The drawings are made in chronological succession by drawing straight on to the film and, as the action progresses, there is always the opportunity for improvisation. McLaren however does not depend on chance. He prepares a careful continuity of action development, and makes sure that the theme of the film based on a visual idea, should not be lost. Here, continuity leans heavily on the sound track, making full use of the strong beat and rhythmical line of the music. Movement and music blend into a single expression even when the music is used as a counterpoint.

McLaren's process of production is, simply, as follows:

1 Basic idea expressed in rough storyboard.
2 Consultation with the composer.
3 Storyboard revision.
4 Music recording.
5 Music charting. Each beat and phase of the sound track is defined in terms of frame by frame continuity.
6 Final revision of picture continuity, now in terms of the sound track.
7 Transfer of sound track on to dummy roll of clear film. This is then used as the basis for the choreography of the film.
8 Image is drawn on to another clear film (Norman McLaren has constructed a special mechanism which enables him to see the previous image and keep the film in proper register).
9 Drawings advanced frame by frame in succession.
10 Completed drawn film is developed and processed by the laboratory who make two copies; one to synchronise with the sound, the other to use as master release print.

From one of Norman McLaren's latest films *Spheres,*

Saul Bass

A sequence from *The Searching Eye* by Saul Bass and Associates. Saul Bass writes: "Man has devised many different instruments to extend the limits of our "highest privilege" . . . The telescope to penetrate the infinite limits of space . . . the microscope to penetrate the finite limits of matter . . . and the camera, to record what "the searching eye", aided or unaided has found. All learning, the thinking, the doing of man starts first with . . . sight!

The eye, as a tool is part of the equipment of most living organisms. All animal eyes are substantially similar, and in many cases duplicate the human eye. But there is a difference. What is the difference? Animal eyes are used only as a survival tool. The human eye is involved not only with sight . . . but also insight.

Human vision is not only used for measuring and observing, and for establishing cause-effect relationships . . . but also to endow or transform objects through the imagination . . . to recall the past . . . to learn and reconstruct through imitation . . . and for the perception of symbols, as in reading.

Many of McLaren's films also require complex optical and special effects, which are obtained from the master material.

11 Finished print is viewed and colour corrections made.

Not all McLaren's films follow the same procedure, but they are all carefully preplanned and consequently need little or no alteration or revision during the physical production. It is an accepted fact with Norman McLaren that the more complete the development of a sequence and the closer the visual changes from one frame to another, the greater the need for preproduction planning.

SAUL BASS

Saul Bass is one of the few artists able to use his skills in a number of media—live action, animation, special effects and a combination of all three. He brings these techniques together with a keen sense of graphic organisation and control. Then there is another value which endows the Bass touch—this is the intelligent use of visual symbols which are instantly identifiable; like the shape of the tear drop in his title for the feature film *Bonjour Tristesse.* He has a sharp instinct for defining forms in their most basic element, i.e.

circular, triangular, square and linear shapes. From these elements he advances his visual theme, rather as a computer works out rhythmical lines in a musical fugue. From the basic shapes a theme emerges which, as it develops, acquires an intellectual statement. The visual theme is varied but not lost in the process of development, becoming enriched with other elements involved in his film—movement, time progression, music and voice. The latter is never organically absorbed with the other values as is the case with Norman McLaren. The visual continuity and variety are always surprising and are indefinably based on visual creative ideas. The results provide a rich experience for the audience emotionally as well as aesthetically as, for instance, in the case of *From Here to There* and *The Searching Eye*, films which mainly use live action.

Most of Bass's other work is mainly feature film titles in which visual metamorphosis leads to a visual statement. The titles establish the basic content and theme of a film and create the right mood for the audience in addition to being in themselves an entertaining spectacle using a different visual medium from the film itself. They give the essential credits in a short, concise and imaginative way which inevitably impart high prestige to the film.

The story is thus, of the eye (and his meaning of human vision), and of a boy who is at the beginning of his use of this great tool . . . A world of experience and knowledge through vision awaits him . . . a world already known to adults. He will reach and extend the boundaries of that world because he will by his nature, keep looking . . . pushing . . . to the limits of his understanding at every given moment. We are with him for these few moments . . . at this time . . . and at this place . . .

Sequence from the film *From Here to There.* Designed by Elaine and Saul Bass. Produced by Saul Bass & Associates for United Air Lines Inc. The film deals, in kaleidoscopic form, with the human experience of travel . . . the excitement, the love, the poignancy . . . of partings and greetings . . . and the unique visual experience of aerial flight.

Saul Bass is a first class example of the highest order of directorial discipline. He never loses sight of the basic objective of a film despite the various methods of filming used, and makes a careful choice in his team of scriptwriters, camera operators and animators. Each area of activity requires the utmost skill in the chain of events leading to the finished product. Bass's teams have both visual sense and technical competence.

The storyboard is a most important stage in Bass's films. It is one aspect of production which he prefers to do himself. At this point practically all the problems requiring a visual solution are solved and the work already shows the preliminary development of a storyline in terms of imaginative use of moving pictures.

The subsequent stages of work enable the flow of continuity to be smooth and ensure that the end product is of the highest technical quality.

So, although both McLaren and Bass depend on visual themes, their work methods are very different. McLaren mostly works alone while Bass works with a carefully selected team. The latter therefore, is bound to be broader in script content and technical range.

One of the latest Bass productions before his first feature film 'Phase 4 (1974) is a documentary *Notes on Change* which deals with the impact and velocity of change, and its effects on the lives of ordinary Americans. The theme is broad and penetrating, obviously demanding an expert scriptwriter who in this case is Mayo Simon. Bass's capabilities lie in his ability to translate the script's literary elements into exciting visual continuity and the application of the most up to date techniques such as time-lapse, aerial image, underwater, multi-image and stop motion photography.

The style of animated films could be divided into two regions. The western hemisphere comprising of the North American continent but including Japan, and the Eastern Hemisphere which is the European Continent with strong emphasis on the work of central and eastern European countries. It is however important to point out that there exists a duplication and overlap between the work of the two hemispheres which is due to a process of influences which regions constantly exert on one another. A further reason for overlap lies in the fact that communication between animation artists nowadays is frequent through the medium of film festivals in Annecy (France) and Zagreb (Jugoslavia) where often as many as 500 to 600 animators show and exchange their work. Animated films also travel fast and far. Since most animated films are short and contain little dialogue they tend to over-ride national barriers. Many are seen on television since it is easy to understand or translate them into another language. The main difference arises from an outlook on life itself.

THE WESTERN HEMISPHERE

Animated films in the western hemisphere are influenced by a commercial outlook whereby the end product must be a saleable commodity in a high competitive 'advertising' field. The public acceptance is of primary consideration and the influence of the sponsor who puts up the finances for a film project may be the deciding factor and the last word. The film has certain conditions to fulfil in order to be made. In the United States and in Japan the two largest markets in the world of films have two specific objectives to achieve. One, to sell a product by direct persuasion in form of a short TV spot; two, to sell a product by goodwill through entertaining the audience during the programme period itself with entertaining specials or series. In both cases the advertiser pays a lot of money for the privilege, failure of the operation would be too expensive, and the advertising agency would be unlikely to choose a loser again. The difference between the budget of short spot (direct sale) and long entertainment productions (indirect sale) is dramatic in favour of the short spots. Consequently the longer films become verbally based exercises of compromise between what was known as animated movies sometime ago, compared with today's style based on static changes of still poses whereby the characters only mimic the pre-recorded dialogue, and perform a limited amount of repeated motion. There is, however, a better possibility of exposing new ideas in graphic design and techniques in the shorter TV spots. These values could contribute to the overall impact of such films wherein this 30–60 seconds duration provides them with a high rate of memory retention. The dominant contribution of the long entertainment films is the storywriter. He is often

an experienced gag writer and knows how to develop a comedy situation. He writes fast and also very often forgets that animation has its own laws of evolution. Visualisers have substantial problems in translating such verbal scripts into the medium of animation. There is a crying need for a new breed of writer who could express himself in terms of visual images or be able to combine the elements of dialogue and verbal expression with the visual end product. Such a skill corresponds with the ideas advanced by Eisenstein in the 1930's when referring to the relationship of the two disciplines. The success of this approach is some concern to the animation, the television and also the advertising industry. It is interesting to notice that while visual communication expanded so rapidly in our times, the attitude hardly changed with it. Spoken words remain dominant in longer films, and they so remain even in the more expensively produced TV specials of half-hour and one hour length, a format which has been in fashion during the nineteen-seventies.

It would be rather unfair not to refer to the work of the 'National Board of Canada' and the number of independent film makers in the U.S.A. and Japan who have succeeded in developing their own visual style away from the more popular commercial productions of Hollywood. The animation unit at the N.F.B.C. have distinguished themselves with Norman McLaren's lifetime contribution of experimental films, which without exception are based on pictorial development. So are many other artists from the same stable like Ryan Larkin who made the film *Walking* shown in these pages, and Mike Mills who directed *Evolution* also represented here. Neither of these productions depends on commentary. On the other hand Grgic's *Hot Stuff* does depend on narration, but the film is a masterly example of how voice and picture can be punctuated for the best effect. The voice is used to motivate a situation which is taken over by the characters in the form of their reaction and behaviour. The action never duplicates the narration which is written to emphasise the behaviour of characters and bridge over the episodes. The three levels—voice, action, sound effects, are expertly integrated, and help to give meaning to the visual ideas. The film promotes fire precaution with a formidable force of conviction.

The work of young American film makers falls into several distinct categories, most of which reflect the tone and the nature of the social order in which this generation are confronted. The first type is concerned with the illustration of popular jazz music and American folk songs, using the present trend of *art-nouveau* graphic style. One of the best examples of this trend is Barry Nelson's *Keep Cool*, a tale of a coloured jailbird escaping from prison, and shooting his old unfaithful sweetheart just to be captured again. This sad tale, and orchestrated song in fine style by Oscar Brown Jnr., is animated with excellent continuity,

Mike Mills (Canada)

Full storyboard from *Evolution* by Mike Mills. Mills, a highly talented animator assisted John Halas in London before going to Canada to work for the National Film Board of Canada. His film *Evolution* is a short history of life. It won an award at the Annecy Film Festival.

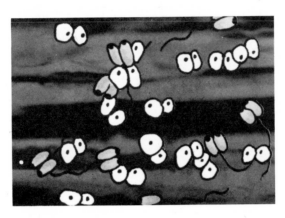 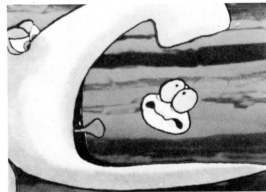

A SHARP SMILE

Antti Peranne (Finland)
The Smile. A Studio 'A' production in Tapiola, Finland. Script and direction by Antti Peranne.

and is a typical example of this new genre. Not so successful in style, but just as lively and popular is the feature film *Fritz the Cat* which attempts to reflect the permissive sexual attitude of the west; also, using pop art graphics, which however has been aired in several TV commercials as well as in the Beatle's film *Yellow Submarine*. Both the Fritz films and *Heavy Traffic* (the same stable) succeed in communicating a contemporary attitude with a contemporary style but primarily retain their identity as typical American films

communicating with the sophisticated young generation of the western hemisphere. These films have some difficulties of acceptance in the eastern European countries on account of their open attitude, violence, and brash sound track. They are however, following faithfully the path which has already been laid to win adult audiences to animation by *Animal Farm*, *Mr. Wonderbird* and *Yellow Submarine*. The approach of the script is original, and apart from the open streak of commercial exploitation of today's semi-pornographic market those new features from the United States have some merits—they are well written and competently drawn and animated.

A further type of film production both in the U.S.A. and Japan is the work of individual experimental film makers. These films are totally visual and only accompanied by music and sound effects Some are generated by the aid of computer. In spite of the fact that such films are not group efforts, the existence of predetermination of what the next frame and scene should contain would be useful for the film maker. In the case of computer generated film, it is unavoidable that the creator would prepare his flow chart in order to process his programme through the machine. For instance in the work of John Whitney who uses an IBM digital computer for his films each frame would be preplotted in the way of a musical score. Practically nothing is left to chance effects. Other computer systems like the 'Scanimation' may allow wider flexibility of visual expression. Among the many hundreds of films which are produced annually in the U.S., Adam Beckett's *Flesh Flows* may be the

Sigondo Bignardi (Italy)
Tout Reque by Sigondo Bignardi. The film's style is strongly influenced by Oriental decorative art.

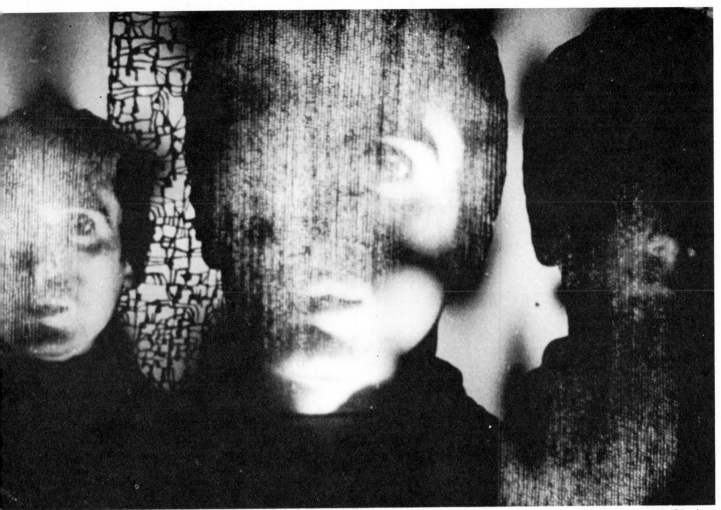

Piotr Kamler (France)

Labyrinth by Piotr Kamler. An experimental film and an attempt to visualise man's inner emotions. The film combines live action with texturised animation.

John and Faith Hubley (U.S.A.)

Of Man and Demon by John and Faith Hubley. A dramatic and charming tale of how man overcomes the evils of pollution. Made for IBM.

most interesting experiment. The film uses partial computerised visualisation to express the climax of a sexual experience. The film was carefully preplanned.

It is gratifying to notice that film makers of outstanding talent like John Hubley in New York Morton and Milton Goldsholl in Chicago, Jeff Hale and Derek Lamb (both born in England) in San Francisco, and Sam Weiss and Fred Wolf in Los Angeles, continue to maintain their high standards in spite of considerable commercial pressures.

Sam Weiss and Nick Bosustow's *The Legend of John Henry* a film based on John Henry, a coloured American folk hero, is especially notable for its design, up to date treatment of animation, good sound track, the song by Roberta Flack, and for the development of the ballad's theme into a strong dramatic climax.

From Japan, Yoji Kuri continues to make purely visual based films from his own comic strip cartoons, writing his own scripts. Kuri's films have a perfect balance of scriptic ideas, drawings, animation and sound. The problem of scripting experimental films is minimised by the fact that the artist is not obliged to communicate his ideas to another person. If he is working with a small group they usually work in close collaboration. His continuity problem however remains. He has to make a prejudged decision of what the next frames and scenes should be. Few are able to carry these factors in their mind, and create pictures as they go along.

Any artist working in films and television has to face up to the fact that his work is conceived in terms of time continuity. All work in the fluid medium has a beginning and an end. The question is what to put in the middle.

Gerald Potterton (Canada)

Last to Go based on a short play by Harold Pinter. Potterton is one of the leading independent producers in Canada. He started with John Halas and Joy Batchelor in London, working on *Animal Farm*.

Gerald Frydman (Belgium)

Scarabus by Gerald Frydman. A surrealistic film in the tradition of Belgium surrealist art which is successfully transferred into another dimension.

Axel Jahn (West Germany)

Between Dreams by Axel Jahn has a strong surrealistic influence with a multimedia approach.

Raoul Servais (Belgium)

To Speak or not to Speak by Raoul Servais. A philosophical statement on the liberty of man, the film is made in a most interesting style.

Emanuele Luzzati and Giulio Gianini (Italy)

An Italian in Algiers by two out-standing Italian designers who made an impace with their colourful interpretation of the opera.

Vera Linnecar, Keith Learner and Nancy Hanna (U.K.)

I'm Glad you asked that Question made by the above for the British Gas Council.

Zlatko Grgic (Yugoslavia)

Hot Stuff by Zlatko Grgic made while he was working for the National Film Board of Canada, A film made for the Dominion Fire Commission on fire safety.

123

Pavel Prochazka (Czechoslovakia)

The Preacher by Pavel Prochazka who worked for the World Council of Churches in Geneva for whom he made this film.

Legend of John Henry. A film based on the coloured hero of John Henry, directed by Sam Weiss and produced by Nick Bosustow and David Adams for Pyramid Films, U.S.A.

A. Garols

gor E L'Erba Musicale. Part of an
⸱lian television series directed by
A. Garols for Audiovisivi Demas
⸱.l. in Milan.

Best Friends story and direction by
Don Arioli and Bob Browing of
Canada. Film produced by the
National Film Board of Canada.

Henry 9 to 5 by Bob Godfrey (G.B.).
A satire showing the sex dreams of a
typical London commuter leaving no
energy for the night.

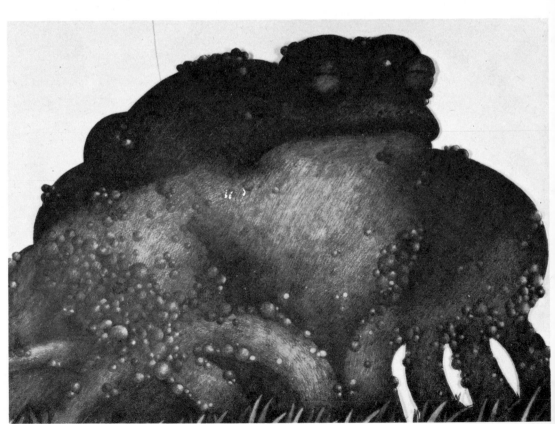

Frog and the Fairy. Story and direction
by John Halas (G.B.) design by
Wayne Anderson.

Farce Anthropo Cynique. Story and direction by Kihachiro Kawamoto, Japan. A remarkable film using surrealistical ideas and clever transitions. A welcome new talent from Japan.

Pegasus by Raoul Servais, Belgium. A dramatic story with strong graphics.

La Planete Sauvage. This feature length science fiction film directed by Rene Laloux and designed by Roland Topor, France, was animated in Czechoslovakia.

rth Keeping by Goldsholl Asso-
ites, U.S.A., in Chicago. This most
ented team shows the effect of
lution on the globe.

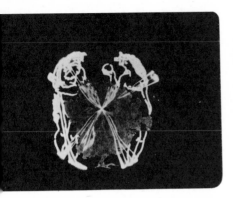

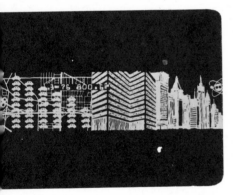

V.S.—I

THE EASTERN HEMISPHERE

Films produced in the eastern hemisphere differ from the west in a great number of ways. In their outlook, in their objective, in their visual style and often in their ultimate use. But the most important difference exists in the fact that they are primarily conceived in visual terms. Narration is seldom used, and dialogue is minimised to basic essentials. As a rule they are not timed so expertly as an average film from the U.S.A. and from a technical point of view they may be less expertly executed. However, they contain a greater number of visually based ideas. While there are a great number of films specially made for children, those which are not intended for them tend to have a more mature outlook and are aimed at intelligent audiences. Large numbers of films are being produced and are of an experimental nature with up to date graphics. Fine arts have their influence as well. Many Polish films are painted under the photographic camera, as in the film *Horse* by Giercz and *Mimosa* by Gzpakowicz. The element of pictorial brilliance, movement and sound are fused in these films creating a new type of filmic approach to the fine arts. Object animation with materials like wood, paper and plastics are also tried out. Czechoslovakia and Russia are rich with artists using such materials. Bretislav Pojar in Prague and Serebrakov in Moscow have made films of the highest quality with three dimensional marionettes.

Many films from Yugoslavia and Hungary contain a sense of gaiety and humour derived from visual jokes which are extended with lively and spirited animation. They are typical of the humour of central Europe. These films could not be made anywhere else. A bitter outlook on life is sharply evident in them. The satire provides the relief. Good examples of this genre are films made by the Yugoslav Nedeljko Dragic in his films *Tup-Tup* and *Diary*. B. Dovnikovic from Zagreb in his film *Traveller Second Class* uses as his centre character a typical European citizen in the train who has to endure the discomfort of primitive local transport. Imagination runs high in the treatment of this film, which is pointed with observations and highly amusing in the meantime. There is no dialogue, the film is carried by action. So it is in the Czechoslovac Vaclav Bedrich's film *Automatic* which is a film about the conflict between man and machine.

The Hungarian, Marcell Jankovics in his film *The Water of Life* shows a similar repressed character driven to suicide by the smoothest everyday occurrences but not competent enough to succeed. In his other short film *Sisyphus* Jankovics, with a few brush strokes, containing the outlines of a figure heaving an enormous boulder, is able to express such power and dynamism that only masterly handling of animation can achieve.

Not all eastern films contain humour. Many are concerned with social injustice, which tends to become heavy. Some, however, like the Polish film maker R. Kijowitz's *Road* contain a fundamental statement with the lightest possible touch. His little figure is at a crossroads, not being able to make up his mind. He himself splits into two halves until at the end of the diversion his split self emerges again into a whole figure. The strength of the idea is carried through with a pointed simplicity. The sound effects are sufficient to reinforce the film without unnecessary doubling up on the visuals with a verbal explanation. Another Polish film entitled *Roll Call* by Ryszard Checkela uses only two words "up—down". The action takes place in a concentration camp. The guard commands the inmates to kneel down and stand up. The command is refused by one of the prisoners. His resistance spreads to all of them. The verbal command on the soundtrack is taken over by the machine gun, which executes them all. The graphics are stark, and dramatic. The mood is sombre.

There is perfect coordination between idea, script, soundtrack and movement adding up to

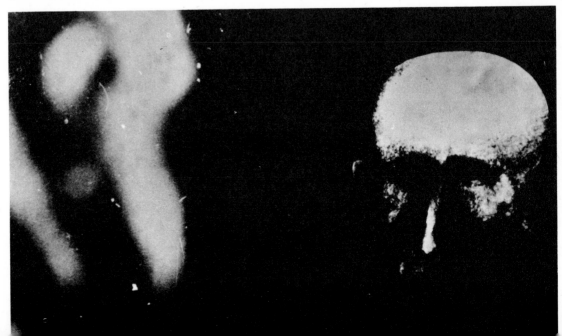

The Wave by Sabin Balasa (Rumania). Mr. Balasa is a painter, applying his art in the three dimensions of moving pictures.

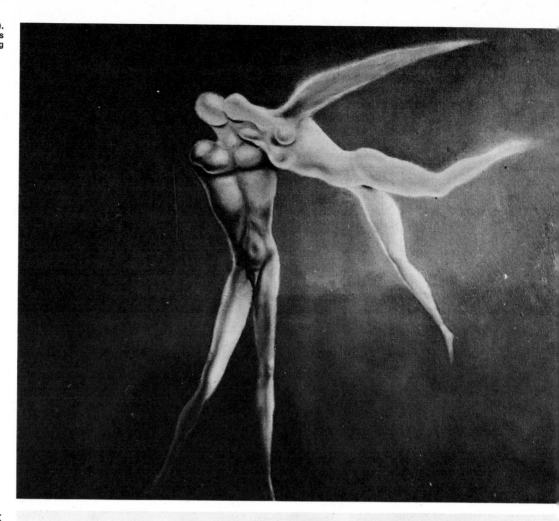

The Engine by Attila Dargay (Hungary). A film about the history of trains.

one of the most powerful expressions of the cinema to date.

Through the work of Donia Donev, Radka Batchvarova, and Todor Dinov, Bulgaria has won much respect in the international field. Their work is typified by telling native stories with charm and simplicity. Dinov's film *The Drum* steps out of this range and employs a combined technique of live photography and animation. It conveys the painful relationship between himself, the artists in live action and his creation in cartoon. It shows a drummer in action, repeated in six different techniques, until the last one, drawn with a drop of blood from his finger provides the last and only acceptable solution.

The Russian scene has changed drastically during the last few years. Classical animation is replaced with a new coat of modern design. Both Boris Stepantsev whose latest work is *The Nutcracker* and Feodor Khitruk employ expert animation, good timing, competently developed storyboards with sophisticated graphic treatment. Khitruk's film *The Island* which was awarded top prizes both in Cannes and Krakow in 1974 shows a character seeking isolation in a confined island, but the influences of technology in the form of modern submarines, ocean liners and jet planes rob him of solitude.

Ivan Ivanov-Vano and Lev Atamanov have proved themselves masters of the craft, through films like *The Battle of Kerzhenets* and *The Ballerina on the Ship*.

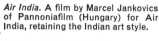

Air India. A film by Marcel Jankovics of Pannoniafilm (Hungary) for Air India, retaining the Indian art style.

Optimist and Pessimist a highly amusing satire by Zlatko Grgic for Zagreb Film, Yugoslavia.

Encyclopaedia of the Executioner
directed by Nicola Majdak for Zagreb
Film, Yugoslavia.

Second Class Passenger written
directed and animated by Borivo
Dovniković, Zagreb Film, Yugoslavia. Won first prize for long films
at the Zagreb Film Festival.

Homo II written by Aleksander Marks
who also directed the film with
Vladmimir Juriša. The film is about
the life cycle of homosapiens.
Zagreb Film production, Yugoslavia.

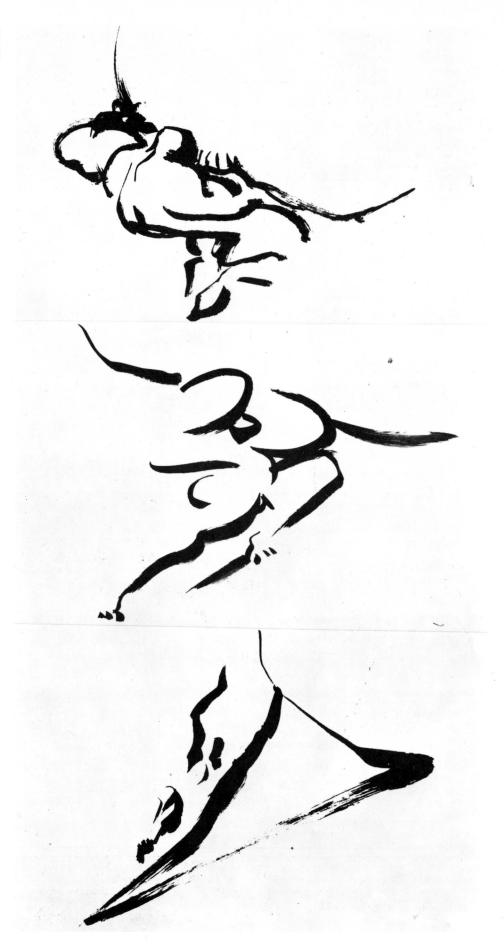

The Direction. Visualisation and direction by Zoran Jovanovic who works and makes films in Belgrade, Yugoslavia.

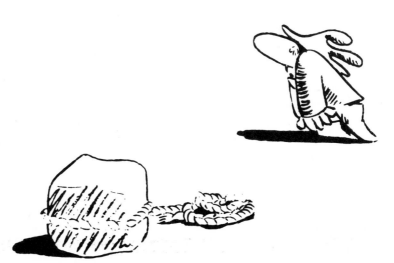

The Water of Life. Script and direction by Marcell Mankovics, Hungary. A satire on suicide.

The Diary by Nedeljko Dragic produced for Zagreb Film, Yugoslavia, and winner of the Grand Prix at the International Film Festival, Zagreb.

The Flower written and directed by Zdzislaw Kudla of Poland.

Island. Script, direction and animation by Feodor Khitruk, the outstanding Russian animator. The film won prizes both at Kracow and Cannes.

The Line by M. Mirmiridis and J. Kousouris, Greece, a film by comparatively inexperienced but talented Greek animators who have just started up in Athens.

The Sound of the Forest directed by Zdziskow Kidka, Poland. The forest comes to life with surealistic objects and figures.

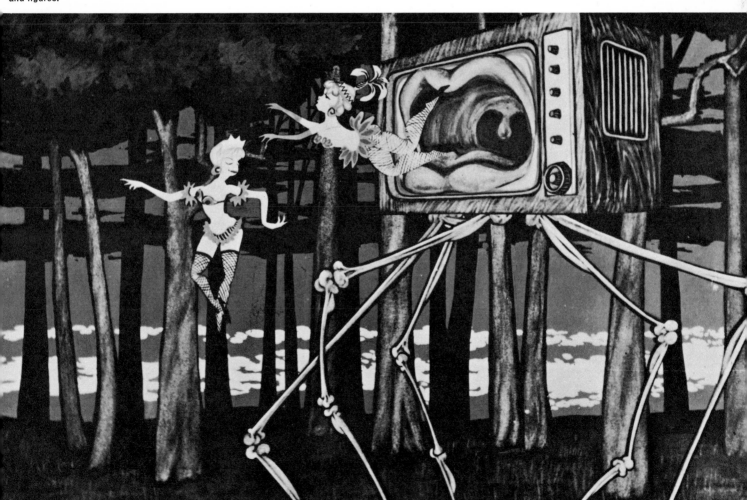

When I was a Kid. Story and direction by Alexander Riesenbuchler, Hungary. A decorative tale of nostalgia.

Just one Drop of Blood by Peter Szoboszlay of Hungary.

The Little Bugler produced by the Shanghai Animation Studios in the Republic of China. It tells the story of a shepherd-boy in the Red Army during the revolutionary Civil War. The style of film is traditional.

THE BRITISH SCENE

The work of the British animators acts as a link between the two hemispheres capable of providing animation of both types. Britain pioneered animation for adult audiences soon after the war. It has led the field for factual, technical and documentary animated films since the beginning of the century. Since the mid-sixties it has been a leading centre in Europe both for sponsored and experimental animation. From the point of view of British style it is based on three characteristic approaches. The majority of films are carried by narrative, either commentary or dialogue or song. A case in point is *Animal Farm* and *Yellow Submarine*. The first feature is based on the literary work of George Orwell and utilises words spoken by animal characters and narration. The later feature is based on pop songs provided by the Beatles. Both features gain by these and both use the element of poetry to provide meaning and clarity for the visuals. Shorter films like Bob Godfrey's *Henry 9 to 5* and *Roobarb* are entirely based on a story delivered by the commentary. The second British characteristic is the matured

humour and sophistication in storytelling. This adult humour is unlike the Continental one which is more down to earth, or the American which is somewhat more direct, far less restrained and faster.

Examples of this approach are films made by the amateur Derek Phillips. His film *The Loser's Club* is about a pessimist, and follows this style like all the other films he has made so far. So is Gerald Scarfe's *The Long Drawn Out Trip*, a brilliantly made satire on American contemporary life. The third value in British animation lies in its consistency of high design standard which is especially evident in George Dunning's work as well as in the work of many hundred film students, who can now practise the art and technique of animation in their colleges. Britain has a bright future in this field through the interest of many thousands of young film makers, and because of its long established tradition of literature which is full of potential subjects for the medium. It also has a flair for abstract thinking which can be transposed to abstract images, as Lewis Carrol and Edward Lear have proved during the last century.

141

CONCLUSION

Visual scripting is an activity of coordinating words with pictures in sequential continuity. The activity is gradually developing into a profession as the demands are rising and visual communication expands. So far, however, there is no professional standard for this practice. There are, nevertheless, a great number of universities and colleges where tuition does take place in scriptwriting although most curricula concentrate on film journalism, documentary and television production, leaving huge gaps in the other media.

It is undoubtedly a difficult field. It requires intelligence in visual literacy, drawing capability, understanding of the bases of movement mechanics and dynamism, understanding of audience reaction as well as the techniques of film making.

The field is still open and practically unexplored.

The relationship between words, pictures, movement, music, sound effects and colour is the greatest keyboard yet that modern technology came to offer to artists. The fluidity and the flexibility of film will be a constant challenge which is likely to attract more and more participants from early age onwards. The exploration of visual poetry and dynamism is still to happen. But the language of *visual grammar* is still to be acquired.

It is inevitable that demand for experienced visual scriptwriters should steadily grow. Sponsored films, long features, television specials, and series, advertising and experimental films need visualising from the start. Without them it is unlikely that these activities can survive. With them they may develop to a new maturity for which we have been waiting a very long time.

The Drum by Todor Dinov, one of the most well-known directors in Bulgaria. His film combined live-action and cartoon production, and expresses the conflicts which face a film maker in his attempt to create.

**THE LIBRARY
OF ANIMATION TECHNOLOGY**

COMPUTER ANIMATION
Edited by John Halas

VISUAL SCRIPTING
Edited by John Halas

FULL LENGTH ANIMATED FEATURE FILMS
(forthcoming)
By Bruno Edera
Edited by John Halas

VISUAL SCRIPTING